a jam-packed gui

*poi*spinning*

illustrated by lucy jane batchelor

written by michal kahn

2

Published by Butterfingers, Devon, England
+44 (0) 1647 441 188
mailbox@butterfingers.co.uk

Cover design and illustrations by Lucy Batchelor.
Tea by mum.

A C.I.P catalogue record for this title is available from the British Library.

ISBN 1 898591 19 9

www.poispinning.com

Printed by Ebenezer Baylis & Son

ACKNOWLEDGEMENTS

It's impossible to thank all those people who contributed to this book by teaching me tricks and giving me ideas. I can only applaud and encourage the generosity and inventiveness of poi spinners in general. Long may it stay that way!

A bunch of people deserve special thanks for doing most of my work for me and lending me lots of pencils:
Miranda Keeling for taking hundreds of photos and then making dinner; Tamara Kahn for taking yet more photos, and for designing all the poi; T.J. Birdi for hours of rendering; Jezz, Monique, Karine and Dimitri for ideas on developing your own style (and for having lots of it!); The talented Guy Bellingham for ideas on choreography and performance; Andrew Batchelor for several hundred insightful discussions of all the topics in this book, and for his design skills; All my students for helping me perfect the ideas in this book on them, and broadening my understanding of the trials of learning poi; Laurie Collard of Butterfingers my patient and supportive publisher; Tim, Drew, Selena, Karine, Sarah, Dimitri and Guy my original and inspiring fellow poisters; Matt Brown, Howie Bailey and Ben Jarlett my housemates, for technical support, moral support, dish-washing support and for letting me pillage their CD collections.

I would also like to thank: Monique Aislabe, Matt Hennem, Rachel O'Kelly, Dylan Keeling, Anna Semlyen, Jim Semlyen, Shawn Ballantine, Ariel Kahn, David Kahn, Gillian Rodgerson, Dave Knox, Paul Dewhurst and Nathan Brown of Oddballs, and Joanne Perry of the New Zealand High Commission.

And most especially Lucy Batchelor for support, advice, cake and humour, and for doing loads more work than she thought she was going to have to do.

Thanks!

This book is dedicated to my much loved and entertaining friends Andrew, Ariel, Ayelet, Ben, Camilla, Daphna, Dylan, Howie, Lindsey, Lowrie, Lucy, Matt, Miranda, Nathan, Noga, Orange, Paul, Rachel, Rad, Sorcha, Shawn, Tamara, Teleika, and Tim.

INTRODUCTION

Welcome to Poi Spinning!

Poi spinning is a beautiful, highly visual performance art in which you create mesmerising patterns of circles around your body, accompanied by much 'ooh!'ing and 'aah!'ing from anyone standing nearby. The circles are created by trails of fabric or fire, attached to the 'poi' which you spin in stunning, complex patterns as you dance.

Contemporary Poi spinning has its roots in the traditional poi spinning of the Maori culture of New Zealand (See page 58), but it's also been influenced by modern dance, contemporary club swinging (page 89) and the boundless inventiveness of the contemporary poisters whose ranks you are soon to join. Thanks to them the art of poi spinning is expanding at an incredible rate that shows no signs of slowing yet.

Because of the sheer number of moves that are out there, this book concentrates on teaching the *central* moves and concepts (from which all others spring), with the aim of freeing you to invent your own tricks and develop your own spinning style. If you're interested in yet more stuff than is explained here explicitly, check out the small print which gives you countless ideas for other moves.

If you are a beginner, start at The Basics section which teaches you all the most important stuff and starts you off gently, building one move on another, so that by the end of the section you'll be spinning some pretty amazing tricks.

If you are not an absolute beginner, just jump to the tricks or topics you'd like to learn. All the tricks are fully cross-referenced, letting you know if there are any other tricks you need to have mastered first, so you can choose your own pattern of learning. The Intermediate section is packed with stonkingly nice moves conveniently arranged in topics so you can get the idea and then invent more of the same. The Advanced section contains...the hard stuff.

If you've got your poi and you're ready to start, open the book flat on the ground, (unless you have a music stand), have a look at the trick and then just go for it. Once you've tried the trick, if you are having problems, check out the problem solvers and helpful hints that are on every page. It's also a good idea to try each trick with each hand on its own first, before trying both hands together, and to learn each move in steps. You might find that a mirror or window helps - especially for those harrowing moments when the poi are behind your head: you'll soon get very used to the path the poi take - even when you can't see them. It's also a good idea to spin your poi very *slowly*. Going slowly gives you time to think, lets you 'feel' the tug of the poi, and takes some of the crunch out of hitting yourself.

Poi has a steep learning curve at the start - within a few weeks you'll have enough spinability to wow your friends - as well as a few bruises. All the same, some tricks will take more time to learn than you expect. For example, the **Behind Your Back** tricks require you to achieve a certain amount of flexibility in your arms and wrists, and other tricks (like the **Alternating** tricks) just hurt to think about. As you work through the book there might be times when you feel that you're finding a particular trick harder to get the hang of than anyone else possibly could! Actually this is a sign that you're progressing just as fast as everyone else. If you are stuck on a trick, give it a good hour of your time, and then take a break and come back to it again the next day: it can make all the difference to just stop thinking about it.

It is totally possible to master all of the tricks in this book, but there's no need to do a trick if you don't like it. The best poi spinning is the spinning *you* enjoy most, and there are big sections in the book on inventing your own moves and developing your own style. If you come up with something incredible, be sure to let me know so it can be included in the next Book of Poi Spinning.

MICHAL KAHN
London, September 2002

CONTENTS

ADVANCED MOVES

APPENDIX

INTRODUCING... THE POI

A poi is really just a weight attached at some distance to your hand. Even a tennis ball in a sock makes a great poi! Here are two of the most common poi and their vital organs:

TAILS

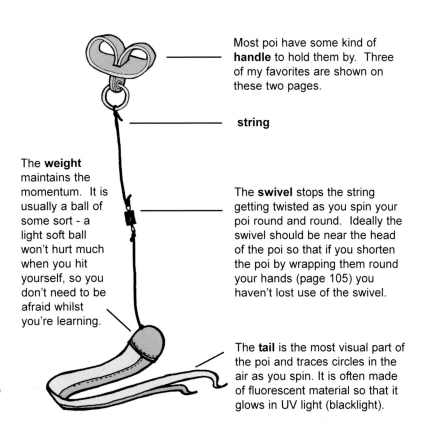

Most poi have some kind of **handle** to hold them by. Three of my favorites are shown on these two pages.

string

The **weight** maintains the momentum. It is usually a ball of some sort - a light soft ball won't hurt much when you hit yourself, so you don't need to be afraid whilst you're learning.

The **swivel** stops the string getting twisted as you spin your poi round and round. Ideally the swivel should be near the head of the poi so that if you shorten the poi by wrapping them round your hands (page 105) you haven't lost use of the swivel.

The **tail** is the most visual part of the poi and traces circles in the air as you spin. It is often made of fluorescent material so that it glows in UV light (blacklight).

A FIRE POI

See Fire Section for more on this type of poi

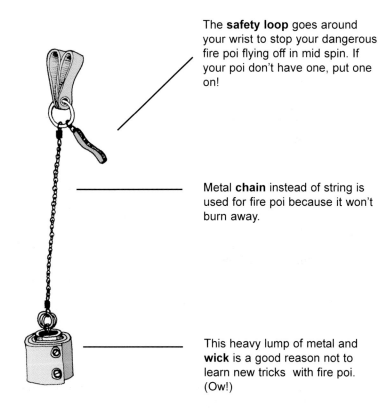

The **safety loop** goes around your wrist to stop your dangerous fire poi flying off in mid spin. If your poi don't have one, put one on!

Metal **chain** instead of string is used for fire poi because it won't burn away.

This heavy lump of metal and **wick** is a good reason not to learn new tricks with fire poi. (Ow!)

HOW TO HOLD YOUR POI

You can hold your poi however you like - just make sure the string hangs down from the *back* of your hand. My favourite ways to hold poi are shown here.

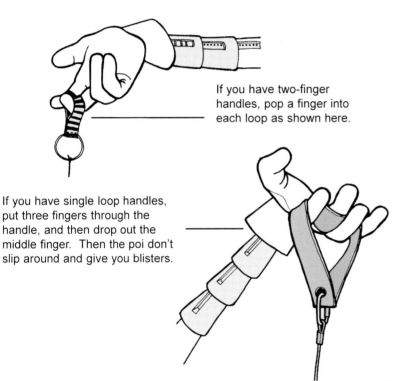

If you have two-finger handles, pop a finger into each loop as shown here.

If you have single loop handles, put three fingers through the handle, and then drop out the middle finger. Then the poi don't slip around and give you blisters.

Relax your fingers but let them curl gently to stop the handle slipping off. You only need to *grip* the handle when you are spinning fire.

HOW LONG SHOULD MY POI BE?

Everyone has different tastes, but if you're a beginner it's useful to have your poi the length from your fingers to your armpit. This lets you do short-string tricks like the Corkscrew (page 93) and it's also easier to learn tricks when your poi aren't too long - but too short and you won't learn to be very neat because your poi will never collide!

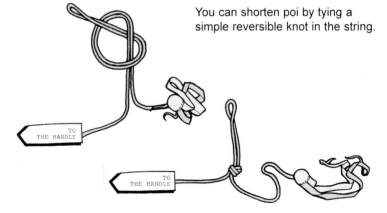

You can shorten poi by tying a simple reversible knot in the string.

Both poi need to be identical in length after you have shortened them, so adjust them by working some string into or out of the knot until they are the same length.

SOME OTHER TYPES OF POI

Stripy Stockings & Ball
If you wear them on your arms your wrist movements are also part of the show and you can spin with open palms which feels great.

Stilt Walking Fire Poi
These are about 1.75m long. You can't do anything too fancy (you really don't want to get tangled in these!) but you make eight circles of fire each time they swing.

Cones
These look very good when doing stills (page 87).

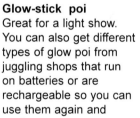

Glow-stick poi
Great for a light show. You can also get different types of glow poi from juggling shops that run on batteries or are rechargeable so you can use them again and again.

Wings
Much easier to use than banner poi and still loads of fabric. Sometimes they look almost like butterfly wings. Aaaaah.....

Banner Poi
Hard work and a bit clumsy, but surround you with waves of rippling fabric - stunning in UV light (blacklight).

Wall of Flame Poi
These poi are made of kevlar fire rope, and make sheets of flame as they spin. Scary!

THE BASICS

SMALL CIRCLES

Right. You're holding your poi properly. Now try spinning some Small Circles, keeping the poi parallel to each other on either side of you.

FORWARDS CIRCLES

BACKWARDS CIRCLES

The poi are spinning in **'parallel time'**, which means they both reach the bottom of their circles at the same time, and you scoop them both up at the same time, keeping them perfectly synchronised all the way round. The other popular rhythm to spin poi in is split time (page 28).

If you find the poi are slanting towards each other, check your arms aren't sticking out to the sides.

Using just your wrists and fingers, scoop the poi up to the top of their circles and then simply let the poi fall back to the bottom, following their path with your fingers. Very slowly spin a few forwards circles without stopping, and then a few backwards circles. Feel the beat of the poi: scoop...scoop...scoop...

As the poi go down, point with your fingers to the place you want them to land. This should correct their path if they're slanting towards or away from each other.

Poi usually spin in one of two planes; the **side planes** or the **wall planes**. It's not that easy at first keeping to the planes (you have to really try to stop your poi slanting out of them) but it'll all feel easy soon. Honest!

THE SIDE PLANES

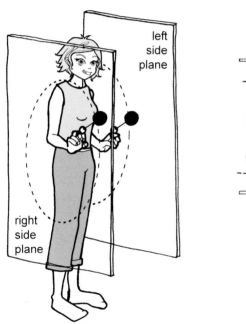

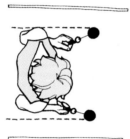

THE WALL PLANES

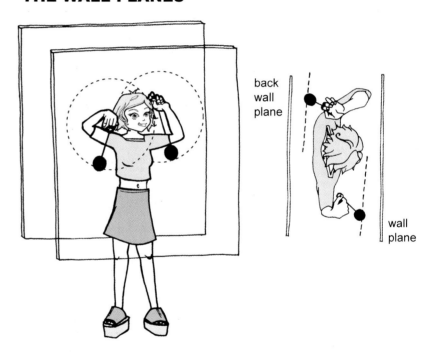

The poi spin parallel to each other, and make flat vertical circles by your sides.

Sometimes, like when you move a poi from one side of your body to the other, you'll need to slant the poi out of the planes a little (see page 34).

The poi spin parallel to each other, and make flat vertical circles in front and behind you.

These two are the main planes for spinning but there's actually an infinite number of planes you could use - see 'other planes' on page 92.

BIG CIRCLES

This one is...um...a big circle. It's spun in the front wall plane.

If your poi are tangling, it's usually because your arms are crossing as you bring the poi back down. Make sure you keep your hands apart. Imagine you are holding a stick between your hands, and you are trying to keep the stick perfectly horizontal the whole way round.

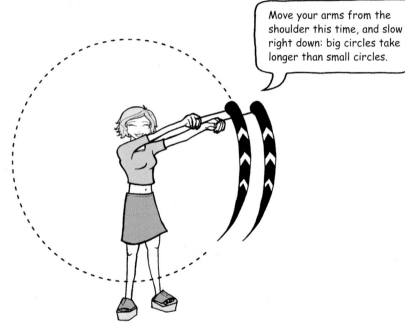

Move your arms from the shoulder this time, and slow right down: big circles take longer than small circles.

Spin the poi in front of you to make a large circle. Start with the poi dangling to one side of your feet. Pull both poi past your feet, up high, and back down to your feet again in one big smooth circle. Have a go at doing a few in a row.

This will help you keep your hands the same distance apart all the time.

Starting with forwards circles, turn 180° and finish by doing some backwards circles. You use a '**carry**' - part of a Big Circle - to link the forwards and backwards circles together. You'll need: **Small Circles**, **Big Circles**.

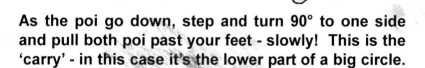

If you have turned 180° by the time the poi come down, they will land on either side of you in backwards circles.

Spin some forwards circles.

As the poi go down, step and turn 90° to one side and pull both poi past your feet - slowly! This is the 'carry' - in this case it's the lower part of a big circle.

As the poi come up, turn some more so you have turned a full 180°. Finish with a few backwards circles.

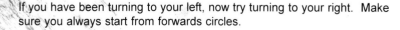

If you have been turning to your left, now try turning to your right. Make sure you always start from forwards circles.

...AND BACK AGAIN

In this move you start off doing backwards circles, turn 180° and end up doing forwards circles. You use a carry (this time the upper part of a Big Circle) to get from backwards circles to forwards circles.

You'll need: **Small Circles**, **Big Circles.**

If you've turned your body enough by the time the poi come down they will fall on either side of your body into small forwards circles.

Begin by spinning a few backwards circles.

As the poi come up, straighten your arms, step to the side and sweep both poi up high.

As the poi go down, turn your body another 90°. Finish with some forwards circles.

Now try linking this turn to the Carry Turn from forwards, so you can turn 360°, or 180° and back again.

The poi don't go behind your head. When you raise your hands up high, they should be above but a little in front of your head.

When you spin in the wall planes, the poi spin in '**inwards**' or '**outwards**' circles. These can be either in front of you or behind you.

One move that uses inwards and outwards circles is the 'Reel'. The poi spin in parallel time, both making a circle in front of you and then a circle behind you in the wall planes. Now, confusingly, although your left hand is spinning outwards circles and your right hand is spinning inwards circles, the poi are going in the same direction (clockwise in this case).

INWARDS CIRCLES

OUTWARDS CIRCLES

From the top of its circle the poi falls in towards your body.

From the top of its circle the poi falls out away from your body.

The poi spin a circle in front of you...

...and then a circle behind you. They pass from in front to behind at the tops of their circles.

Getting your hands to do these different jobs at the same time is hard at first. Turn over and have a look at the step by step instructions for the Shoulder Reel.

The poi spin a circle in front of you and a circle behind you as explained on the previous page. Practice each hand on its own first, using the pictures below. The inwards hand is the hardest - check the pictures to make sure your hand is moving exactly right. Then try the movement step by step with both hands.

You'll need: **Inwards and Outwards Circles**, **Reels**.

It's tough to picture or feel what the poi are doing behind you, so it helps if you watch yourself in a mirror or window.

Let the poi draw the bottom of the circle in front of you by pointing your fingers to the left and then scooping to the right. Your palms face in towards your body.

As the poi come up, turn your hands palm up, fingers pointing behind you and to the left. This pulls the poi diagonally up over your head to come down behind you on the left. As soon as the poi start to go down...

Reels feel awkward at first, even if you're doing it right - it will all feel natural in a couple of weeks as your wrists become more flexible.

Keep the movement in your wrist and fingers - not your arms so much.

Any move you ever do you can also do in 'rewind' - as if you had filmed it and were playing it backwards. It's important to master doing every move both ways. With Reels, this means being able to do Reels with the poi spinning anticlockwise as well as clockwise.

> If you tangle behind, check your hand doesn't go over or behind your head when the poi go behind - your hands should stay on either side of your head (by your ears) all the time.

> It also helps to keep your elbows up and out at shoulder height, and lean back a little as the poi pass behind you.

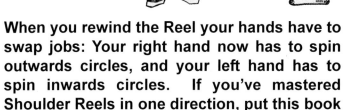

...point the way you want them to go with your fingers - down a bit behind you, and up again on your right. Your palms still face up. As the poi come up...

start to turn your hands palm down, (back to the start position), pulling the poi diagonally over your head back to the start position, and... relax!

When you rewind the Reel your hands have to swap jobs: Your right hand now has to spin outwards circles, and your left hand has to spin inwards circles. If you've mastered Shoulder Reels in one direction, put this book down and teach your hands to do Reels in the other direction.

17

HIP REELS

Like Shoulder Reels, the poi both spin a circle in front of you and then a circle behind you in the wall planes. But *your hands don't make the same movement as in shoulder reels.* Practice each hand on its own first, and then put both hands together in steps.

You'll need: **Inwards and Outwards Circles**, **Reels.**

It's really tempting to let the inwards hand do the same sort of motion as it did in the Shoulder Reel. Don't let it!

Start with both poi next to your right foot.

Scoop the poi up...

...around...

...and down on the left to draw the circle in front of your body.

Your left hand is spinning outwards circles, and your right hand is spinning inwards circles.

The poi pass from in front to behind at the bottom of their circle, not at the top like they did in Shoulder Reels.

You know your inwards hand is doing the right thing if the poi passes *under* your arm as you take it from in front of you to behind you, instead of over.

If the poi hit you on the back of the legs as you bring them in front, you could be bringing the poi forwards too early, whilst they're still at the bottom of their circles.

Scoop both of the poi diagonally past your legs. Your fingers point behind you to the right, and your palms face up.

Scoop the poi up behind you by bending your elbows a little, and flicking your fingers up to try and touch your elbows.

Move the poi in an arc behind you by pointing your fingers up...

...and then down to the left. Now scoop the poi back in front of you taking them diagonally past your legs as in the first picture.

Scoop the poi past your legs, up, around and down all in one fluid motion.

Make sure you teach yourself to do Hip Reels in both directions (clockwise and anticlockwise).

REEL TURN FROM FORWARDS...

Also known as the 'Low Turn'. From forwards circles turn 180° to backwards circles, letting the poi spin a circle behind your hips as you turn. To prepare, try this: spin a forwards circle, and as the poi come up flip your hands as shown so the poi hit you on the back of the head (sorry!). Then try the actual turn.

You'll need: **Small Circles**, **Hip Reels**.

Ow! Preparing for the Reel Turn.

Start with a forwards circle.

Scoop the poi up to hit you on the back of the head, but this time step out of their path by turning 90°, and let them spin an arc behind you. Your fingers move just like in the circle behind you of the Hip Reel.

As the poi come down, step another 90° and scoop them up into backwards circles.

Have a go at doing this turn to the right as well as to the left.

Oof! Preparing for the
Reel Turn.

Also known as the 'High Turn'. From backwards circles, turn 180° to forwards circles, letting the poi do a circle behind your shoulders as you turn. To prepare for this trick, spin a backwards circle, and as the poi go down, put your hands on your shoulders and let your poi hit you on the bum (argh!). Then try the actual turn. Try it to the right and to the left.

You'll need: **Small Circles**, **Shoulder Reels**.

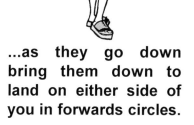

Start with a backwards circle or two.

As the poi go down, put your hands on your shoulders palm up. Step 90° to avoid the poi, (it helps to lean back at this point) and they will spin a circle behind you now that you are out of the way. As the poi come up step another 90° and...

...as they go down bring them down to land on either side of you in forwards circles.

This part of the move is exactly like the circle behind you in Shoulder Reels, so you can move your fingers the same way.

LINKING REELS

To link circles that are far apart - in this case circles by your shoulders and circles by your hips - you use a carry, just as in the Carry Turns (page 13).

You'll need: **Shoulder Reels**, **Hip Reels** (both clockwise).

Slow down for the carry bit - big circles take longer than small circles.

Do some clockwise Shoulder Reels.

As the poi come down in front of you, carry them all the way down to your feet, and...

...take the poi diagonally past your legs and go into clockwise Hip Reels, starting with the circle behind you.

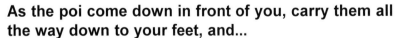

Stretch your arms right across your body as you do the carry bit, to get a nice big flat circle.

Do some clockwise Hip Reels.

As the poi come up past your legs from behind you, carry them up....

...and let them land behind you (your hands palm up on your shoulders) into the circle behind you of a clockwise Shoulder Reel.

LINKING USING THE MATCHING POINT

You can link one move to the next when you find a **'matching point'** - a moment when the position of the poi in one move exactly matches the position of the poi in another move. At this point you can switch between the two moves.

LINKING
CARRY TURNS AND BIG CIRCLES

Do a Carry Turn but stop turning when you reach the carry and do some Big Circles. You can then finish the turn when you get back to the matching point.

LINKING
REELS AND BIG CIRCLES

Do a Hip Reel, and as you do the carry to get to a Shoulder Reel, you can go straight into doing some Big Circles. Then go back to Shoulder or Hip Reels when you reach the matching point.

For some extra pazazz, look at Parallel Pirouettes (page 80) and try linking these to Big Circles.

LINKING REEL TURNS TO REELS

Every time you learn a new move, link it to what you can already do, using a carry or a matching point.

Because the circle behind you in a Reel Turn is the same as the circle behind you in a Reel, you can stop turning at that point and do Reels instead of finishing the turn. To get back to finishing the turn, wait for the circle behind you in the Reel, and continue as you would for the turn.

If you turn to your left, you'll end up doing clockwise Shoulder Reels. If you turn to your right, you'll end up doing anticlockwise Shoulder Reels. If you want to be able to turn both ways, you need to be able to do Reels in both directions.

Now it's up to you to find other matching points so you can link all of the moves you've learnt so far to each other. Try and see if you can link move to move to move without stopping spinning, using either a matching point or a carry.

25

CONTINUOUS TURNS

You can link your turns together but skip the Small Circles, so you are turning continuously. It makes you look like a real pro! You can do this on the same spot, or by stepping sideways as you turn so that you cover ground in a straight line.

You'll need: **Reel Turns**.

You can also try turning to the left for the shoulder bit and then to the right for the hip bit.

Do a Reel Turn from backwards.

Without completing the forwards circle, keep turning to start a Reel Turn from forwards.

As the poi come up you can go straight into a backwards Reel Turn, without doing a backwards circle (picture 2).

Try this with every turn you learn. If you do it with the Carry Turns, you get a Pirouette (page 80). It's particularly flashy with the Split Reel Turn (page 116).

Learning to spin poi is an enchanting and rewarding process in which you develop the graceful ability to narrowly avoid hitting yourself for long periods of time. Admittedly this requires a training period in which you mostly hit yourself.

You *will* develop an ever increasing repertoire of moves and patterns that you can do fluidly. But every time you learn something new, even if you're a pro, you'll end up with impressive bruises. As a consolation, you do get used to it - especially if you don't swing anything too hard and spiky.

If you hit yourself at the same point in a move every time, see if you can work out and correct what's going wrong. Often it's because you are pointing the poi in towards your body. This often happens with **The Weave**. So, try pointing them away from your body a little more. Or it might be because you are moving the poi from one side of you to the other when they are still at the bottom of their path, so that you are pulling them into your body instead of letting them get to the right height to get past you. This often happens with **Reels**. Make sure you are waiting for the poi to be coming up (or going down) to move them from one side to another.

There are also a couple of things you can do to lessen the pain. Try not to learn with fire poi (they hurt a lot more), and if your poi have tennis balls inside, put a few big slashes in each tennis ball so that it becomes less rigid. Careful that you don't end up cutting any chunks out of the ball - slashing a big cross in the bottom of the ball and another couple of big slashes in the sides will be enough. Finally, if you spin very slowly it hurts less - and you'll have more time to think so you end up hitting yourself less if you're learning a move.

To add to the bashings, there's also the tangling. It just comes with the territory: jugglers drop, poisters tangle. Soon you'll be a pro at untangling in a calm, nonchalant fashion, but the odd tangle tantrum is also quite normal! If you're performing you should learn your piece well enough not to tangle, but in case you do, have a prepared plan of action - a comic or dramatic moment, or a way to make it seem part of your piece. If you tangle when your fire poi are alight, put them on the ground with handles far from the wicks and untangle from the handle end.

A final word of warning: be very spatially aware. Don't let yourself dance about with abandon in the vicinity of breakable objects and, more importantly, other people - especially if those people are absorbed in something complicated and destructible (like juggling) that reduces their awareness of you. Unless your poi are highly explosive in which case no one's going to argue with you.

SPLIT TIME

In **split time** the poi take turns to reach the bottom of their circles. The poi are always exactly half a circle apart. So as a result, whenever you spin in split time your poi strings line up along a single line. Split time is also known as 'follow time'.

SMALL CIRCLES

Spin forwards circles in the side planes, and spin them so that the poi take turns to reach the bottom of their circles. The poi are exactly half a circle apart, so the beat becomes right...left...right...left...

You'll need: **Small Circles** (parallel time).

To get from parallel time to split time, just speed up one poi for an instant so that it is half a circle ahead of the other poi. To go back to parallel time again speed up one poi so it catches up the half circle between it and the other poi.

Try doing the same with backwards circles.

These are just like Reels, but the poi spin in split time, so they take it in turns to reach the bottom of each circle. Split Shoulder Reels are shown here - but try the same thing with Hip Reels. The inwards hand leads, reaching the bottom of each circle half a beat before the outwards hand. Make sure you can do Split Reels clockwise *and* anticlockwise. You'll need: **Shoulder Reels**.

> Both poi should have dipped in front before either poi dips behind.

Start with a Shoulder Reel. When the poi are behind your head, pull the inwards poi in front of you a little early so that your poi are now in split time.

The outwards poi dips in front half a circle after the inwards poi.

Keep this rhythm as the poi pass behind you - so the poi spinning inwards dips behind you half a circle before the outwards poi.

The timing is a little odd to get used to: just think right in front...left in front...right behind...left behind.

29

LINKING SPLIT REELS

Split Shoulder Reels and Split Hip Reels are linked using carries. Your hands don't do the carries at the same time but one after the other, staying half a circle apart, which can be a bit tricky at first. One way to link split time reels is shown below.

You'll need: **Split Reels** (both clockwise).

Remember to slow down a little for carries.

From a Split Shoulder Reel, wait 'till your lead poi (the inwards poi) is coming back over your head from behind you.

At that point take it down to hip level in a big carry. As your outwards hand passes over your head from behind you...

...bring it down in a carry. Your lead hand in the meantime starts to do a hip reel by beginning the circle *behind* you.

As the outwards hand reaches your hips, it does a circle *in front* of your hips. You are now doing a Split Hip Reel. Phew!

From Split Hip Reels, find the point when your outwards hand is coming up in front of you. At that point...

...carry your left arm all the way up to Shoulder Reel height.

Let your outwards poi land *behind* you in a Split Shoulder Reel. As the inwards poi comes up from behind you, carry it to your shoulders...

...and let it land in a circle *in front* of your shoulders. You are now spinning Split Shoulder Reels. Does your brain ache?

THE WINDMILL

The Windmill looks...like a windmill. It's exactly like the follow time shoulder reel, except your wrists are touching above your head instead of hovering by your ears.
You'll need: **Split Reels** (shoulder).

The easiest way to get the hang of this is to spin Split Shoulder Reels, and slowly bring your hands together above your head: So put this book down and try doing just that. Your wrists move exactly as they do in the split time Shoulder Reel. The inwards poi leads - it's the first to drop in front and the first to drop behind.

After a bit of practice you should be able to do this with your wrists touching the whole time.

This is simply the Windmill with the circle in front of your head spun as a big circle in split time.

You'll need: **Windmill**.

Careful not to let one arm catch up with the other as you spin the big circle - keep the poi half a circle apart.

Do a Windmill. As the inwards poi comes in front of your head from behind you, carry that arm right across your body and down in a big circle...

...followed by the other poi as it comes over your head from behind you.

As the inwards poi completes the big circle, drop it behind your head followed by the other poi to spin the part of the Windmill that's behind your head.

33

THE WEAVE

BREAKING THE PLANES

When you take the poi from one side of your body to the other, the poi slant out of the plane to get from one side to the other.

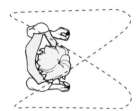

In moves where the poi are constantly passing from side to side, like in the figure of eight shown below or the Weave shown opposite, The poi need to break the plane even when they spin the circle by your side - not just when they are passing from one side to the other. This is so that they don't hit you!

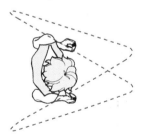

You still want the poi to look like they're spinning in the plane though, so it's best when you first learn the trick to *try* to keep the poi spinning in plane, but if they hit you point them away from your body a bit. This is true for tricks in the wall planes, like Reels, and for tricks in the side planes, like the Weave.

COUNTING BEATS, NOT CIRCLES

When your poi pass from side to side, part of each circle is used to get from one side of you to the other. This means that when you do a figure of eight as shown below, you don't do a complete circle on either side of you. For this reason it's sometimes easier to think in terms of 'beats' instead of circles: in the figure of eight below, the poi spin one beat on each side of you, and two circles in total - but not a complete circle on any one side.

In the Three Beat Weave, shown on the next page, the poi in each hand spin three circles in total, one beat on the near side of your body and two on the far side. Again it's best to think in beats and not in circles, because the downwards part of each circle is used to get to a new position, so there isn't a complete circle in any one place.

Also known as the 'Three Beat Weave', 'Cross-Follow' and the 'Chase', it's a classic poi move, and once you've got it you'll find yourself doing it...a lot. Each hand does three forwards circles in the side plane: one on its own side and two on the far side of your body. Then it comes back to its own side to start again. Practice each hand on its own first. You'll need: **Small Circles** (split time).

Holding just one poi, spin it in a forwards circle.

Let the poi go down on the other side of your body, over your empty hand. Start to spin a forwards circle.

As the poi goes down, take your poi hand *under* your empty hand. As the poi comes up, let it spin another forwards circle, this time under the other hand.

As the poi goes down, bring it back to its own side ready to start again.

When you can do this fluidly, practice the same move with your right hand, letting it spin one circle on your right side and two on your left.

Ready for two hands? Each hand does the three circles explained on the previous page, but the hands weave around each other in split time, making a beautiful pattern that's the same on each side of your body. Try it nice and slow, doing it step by step.
You'll need: **Weave: one hand**.

Make sure the left hand crosses *over* the other hand as the poi comes down, so don't move your right poi too early!

Careful not to take your left hand back to your left side yet - it needs to spin its third circle first.

Swing the left poi in a forwards circle. As the poi goes down...

...let it land on the right side of your body in a forwards circle, just as you did when you were doing one hand on its own.

As the left poi reaches the top of its circle, start the right poi spinning a forwards circle, chasing the left poi on the right side of your body.

As the right poi goes down let it land on the left side of your body in a forwards circle. *The left poi stays on the right side and finishes its third circle.*

PERFECTING THE WEAVE

When you've got the Weave, practice it with your wrists together. This makes the Weave look like a single wheel, as both poi are spinning around the same central point. Use your fingers to point where you want the poi to go, rather than reaching your whole arm.

Let the right poi spin a forwards circle on the far side of you. As the left poi comes down, start to bring it to the same side as the right poi and...

...let the left poi chase the right poi in a forwards circle on the left side of your body. Keep going until your hands have almost recrossed, with your left hand on top.

The right poi stays on the left and spins its third circle. As the left poi comes down, bring it over to the right side...

...followed by the right poi as the right poi comes down. Now back to picture 3.

When you think you have it, check again. It's fairly usual to get it right on one side of your body and not on the other. The circle people usually miss out is the third circle.

THE GIANT WEAVE

There's only one circle on each side of the Weave that's easy to make big, and it adds a moment of drama to the weave. No circles are added to or missing from the Weave - it's just that one of the circles is really big. Here the big circle on your right side is shown - but you can also do it on your left.

You'll need: **Weave**.

Do the Weave, and find the moment where your right hand is about to come back to your right side.

As your right hand comes to your right side and your arms uncross on your right, stretch your arms out in a big circle, stretching your right arm back and your left arm forwards so that your hands are really far apart.

As you finish the big circle, let your right hand cross over your left hand...

...to the left side of your body, so you are now spinning the Weave again (picture 4 of the Weave).

Slow right down for the big circle, and turn your right shoulder back as your right hand goes back so your right poi can spin in the side plane.

Try this with the Backwards Weave too, doing the big circle as your hands uncross on each side.

This is the Weave in 'rewind', as if you'd filmed the Weave and were playing it backwards. It's the same as the Weave except the poi spin backwards and your hands cross *under* each other instead of over. Each poi still spins one circle on its own side and two on the far side, and the poi spin in split time. Try each hand on its own first.

You'll need: **Small Circles** (split time).

Spin the poi in a backwards circle. As the poi comes up...

...take it to your right side so that it spins a backwards circle *under* your right hand.

As the poi comes up, take your left hand out from under your right hand to over your right hand...

...and let the poi go down to spin a circle over the *top* of your right hand on the right side of your body.

As the poi comes up, bring it back to your left side, ready to begin again.

When you're ready, practice this same move with your right hand, letting it spin one circle on the right side and two on the left side of your body.

Your left hand makes exactly the same motion to spin the third circle as it did to spin the second circle. Check you're not contorting your hand too much to spin this last circle.

THE BACKWARDS WEAVE

Also known as the 'Reverse Weave'. When you can do this move, you open doors to some really fabulous spinning - the Fountain for example. Mastering it can be a little trickier than the Weave because backwards circles feel a little less natural than forwards circles. Try learning the trick in steps. You'll need: **Backwards Weave: one hand.**

> You need to bend your wrists and fingers when the poi is on the far side of your body to get the poi to spin in the wall plane.

Spin a backwards circle with your left poi on your left side. As the poi comes up...

...get it to pass behind your right poi so that it starts to spin a backwards circle under your right hand on your right side.

Once you've got the hang of the Backwards Weave, try getting into it from Small Circles (backwards) in split time.

As your left poi starts to go down on your right side, chase it with your right poi.

Your hands will uncross on your right. Keep both poi on your right as your hands start to recross with your right hand now underneath. As your right poi comes up...

Check you aren't missing out your right hand's third circle - or the third circle your left hand makes in the last picture.

Bring your left hand *low* to get it to cross under. If you lift your right arm *up* to get your left hand to cross under, you'll soon end up spinning by your head! So whenever a hand crosses under, bring it a bit lower.

...let it cross under your left hand to your left side. Your left poi is still on your right, finishing its third circle.

As your right poi drops in to a backwards circle on your left, bring your left poi to your left side, chasing your right poi...

...so your hands uncross on your left...

...and recross. As your left poi comes up, let it cross under your right hand to your right side, leaving your right poi to do its third circle on your left. Now back to picture 3.

When you are happy with your Backwards Weave, try to get it so you can do it with your wrists touching all the time, just as you did with the Weave.

DEVELOPING YOUR STYLE

Right, time to have some fun!

Near the beginning of your poi career is the best time to start to explore getting the maximum from each move. Have some playtime, and just muck around with a move to find more fun or expressive ways of doing it. Choose one move and do it for at least five minutes, seeing how you can move with it, dance with it (pop some music on if you want to), vary it, and get it to be expressive or funny. This is the first step in developing your own style, and will stop you becoming a purely mechanical poi spinner. If you're stuck for ideas, try a few of these variations:

Change the *speed* you are spinning at, perhaps for just a couple of beats, perhaps speeding up or slowing down gradually over a longer period. (Speeding up to a ferocious pace always gets a clap with fire poi - especially if you make it look like hard work!)

Move the pattern up or down **- try it high over your head or down by your knees.**

or *move your body up or down*- **kneel, jump, lie down...**

Walk, skip, side step **- come up with some graceful ways of moving with your trick - and some funny ones. Don't be shy now!**

Put some *big circles* in anywhere you can.

Experiment with different *stances and postures*. Then try exaggerating them.

Try a few of these variations at the same time - for example walk whilst taking a move up and down, spinning faster as you take it up.

Try portraying different emotions whilst spinning - either for comedy value or in all seriousness. Some ideas are: submissive, threatening, flirtatious, angry, excited, shy, friendly, sad, proud. You can always tap into the way you feel right now. Think of both your body and your poi: how do you move, what stances are appropriate, what does your face do, how fast do your poi spin, what sounds do you make...ahem...fight the embarrassment!

WEAVE TURN FROM FORWARDS...

Whenever you do a turn, you are effectively linking two moves together: in this case you are linking the Weave to the Backwards Weave. From the Weave, you turn 180° whilst doing some hocus pocus with your hands and end up doing the Backwards Weave. It helps if you say the magic word.

You'll need: **Weave**, **Backwards Weave**.

Make sure your hands have re-crossed before you turn the last 90°.

Start with a forwards Weave. Find the point at which your right hand goes over the top of your left hand to spin a forwards circle on your left. Now...

...turn your body 90° to the left as your right hand goes over your left. Then...

...uncross your hands, and...

...recross them, turning 90° as your right hand crosses under your left hand to spin a backwards circle on your left. You are now in a Backwards Weave (picture 5, page 41).

Starting from a Backwards Weave, you turn 180° whilst twiddling your poi a bit, and as if by magic end up doing the forwards Weave.

You'll need: **Backwards Weave**, **Weave**.

Make sure your hands have re-crossed before you turn the last 90°.

Do a Backwards Weave and find the point where your right hand comes up under your left hand to spin a circle on your left. At this point...

...turn 90° to your left as your right hand comes up under your left...

...uncross your hands...

...and recross them. As your right poi comes down on top, take it over to your left side as you turn 90°. You're now doing the Weave (picture 4, page 36).

NON-TURNING TURNS

You can do any turn *without* turning your body. Presto! Instantly the move becomes a static trick. Actually, you still move your torso as you do in the usual turn, but you keep your feet and head pointing one way to give the impression that you're not turning. Here it's shown with a Weave Turn. You'll need: **Weave Turn from forwards**.

When you do the Weaves in this position, it helps to turn your torso, reach far over your shoulder and point the poi away from your body when they are behind you so you don't hit yourself.

GETTING INTO IT...

THE NON-TURNING WEAVE TURN

Do the Weave. Still doing the Weave in the same point in space...

...turn your legs and head 90° to the left, to get ready to do the non-turn, and...

... as your right hand crosses over to the left, do the Weave Turn exactly as you usually do it, but without moving your feet or head. You finish in a Backwards Weave that is in the same awkward place as the Weave you started with, but on the other side of your body.

Try this with the Weave Turn from backwards, and with any other turn that you like: it works for every turn there is!

The Fountain is a breathtaking move. You spin a big circle made up of loads of little circles with fluid effortlessness. It's just amazing how your hands don't get tangled! And, it's not as hard as it looks. Alright!

There's many different moves poisters call the Fountain. All involve doing small split time circles round the edge of a big circle. I've shown my favourite one here. This picture is an artist's impression to give you the general idea - it doesn't show, for example, which circles are behind which, so to learn the move turn over!

FOUNTAIN

It's really just a Non-Turning Weave Turn from forwards done whilst reaching down, linked to a Non-Turning Weave Turn from backwards done whilst reaching up. Practice it in two halves, and then follow the instructions on linking the two halves together at just the right moment.

You'll need: **Non-Turning Turns**.

FIRST HALF

Do a Non-Turning Weave Turn from forwards, but this time as your right hand goes down over the top of your left hand...

...reach it all the way down as low as you can go.

Stay low as your hands uncross, and as your right hand comes up under your left...

...reach it up so you are back at normal Weave height - about chest level, and doing the Backwards Weave.

SECOND HALF

Do a Non-Turning Weave Turn from backwards, but as your left hand comes up under your right...

...reach it up as high as you can.

Keep your poi really high as your hands uncross, and as your left hand crosses over your right hand...

...reach it back down so you end up doing the Weave at its normal height.

Make sure your hands have re-crossed before you start the Weave.

The 2nd half can also be used to link the Weaves to the Windmill at picture three, which is a 'matching point' (page 24) with the Windmill.

If you want an extra challenge, try turning 360° whilst doing the Fountain - if you just go for it it will probably work after a couple of tries.

LINKING THE TWO HALVES TOGETHER.

OK, ready to put it together? All you do is the first half and then the second half (then the first half again if you want to keep on going!), but each time you start the next half at the soonest opportunity. So you start to turn from forwards *the first time* your right hand goes over the top of your left hand, and you start to turn from backwards *the first time* your left hand comes up underneath your right hand. It helps to think of yourself as reaching for four points: chest height on your right for The Weave, low down by your legs, chest height on your left for the Backwards Weave, and up high over your head.

SMALL CIRCLES

So far the poi have always been going in the same direction - either both forwards, both backwards, both clockwise or both anticlockwise. But you can also spin them so they are going in **opposite directions**: one forwards and one backwards, or one clockwise and one anticlockwise.

The poi spin in Small Circles in the side planes in parallel time, but one poi spins forwards whilst the other spins backwards.

You'll need: **Small Circles** (page 10).

Try this with your right hand spinning forwards, and your left hand spinning backwards, and vice versa.

Spin one poi backwards, and then start the other poi spinning forwards. They both reach the bottom of their circles at the same time.

The poi spin in parallel time - they both reach the bottom of their circles at the same time. 'Parallel' is not the best word to use to describe this timing when the poi are spinning in opposite directions, because in some senses the poi are not spinning in parallel.

Some people use '**counter time**' to mean 'parallel time in opposite directions' so as to avoid this problem. Here I've stuck to using 'parallel time' because it's still the consensus.

The poi spin large circles in opposite directions in the side planes, so you use your whole arm. Definitely get the hang of this one without your poi first.

Turning your shoulders lets the arm behind you keep in the wall plane.

Start with your arms by your sides, your shoulders facing forwards. As you bring one arm back behind you and one arm up in front of you...

...turn your shoulders towards the arm that is behind you.

As your arms come up above your head, turn your shoulders back to face forwards.

Let the arm that came up in front drop down behind, and the other arm drop in front. Turn your shoulders a little towards the arm behind you...and back to the start (picture 1).

THE BUTTERFLY

The poi spin a circle in opposite directions (in this case both spin inwards) in the same place as each other, giving the impression that they are making just one circle between them.

You'll need: **Inwards and Outwards Circles**.

GETTING INTO IT

INWARDS BUTTERFLY

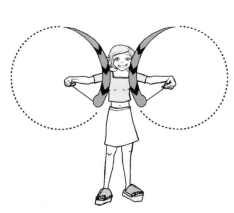

Start with some inwards circles. Get the planes really flat, and then...

...get one hand higher than the other. Each time the poi go down bring your hands closer together until...

...one hand is exactly on top of the other. Now simply bounce your hands down as the poi go down...

...and up as the poi come up. You don't need to do anything with your wrists or fingers. Keep it going: bounce... bounce... bounce...

It's usually your dominant hand that you raise higher, to go on top in the inwards Butterfly - your right hand if you are right handed.

SIDE VIEW

One hand should be directly above the other, as if you are holding a vertical stick between both hands.

From this side view you can see that when the poi are at the bottom of their circle, the poi in the top hand is in front. When the poi are at the top of their circle, the poi in the lower hand is in front. So as you bounce your hands up and down you will need to angle them a little to let this happen.

Once you can do it, there's no need to go through the 'getting into it' each time - just go straight into the Butterfly.

OUTWARDS BUTTERFLY

Now try an outwards Butterfly. Get into it in the same way, but spin *outwards* circles, and put the hand that was on top for the inwards Butterfly *underneath*. When you spin the Butterfly, your hands need to be directly on top of each other, bouncing up and down. Try to move your fingers only a little.

BEHIND THE BACK BUTTERFLY

You can also try doing the Butterfly behind your back, either inwards or outwards. This is a bit tangleful! It helps if you keep one hand closer to your body than the other, curl your fingers so the poi strings don't get caught on them, and tip your head forwards so you don't hit the back of your head.

ANGEL WINGS: INWARDS

Also known as the 'Overhead Butterfly', this is an inwards Butterfly in front and then one behind your head. Keep to the beat of the poi as you do this. You don't need to move your wrists or fingers at all and it will still work! Keep your wrists together the whole time. You'll need: **Butterfly** (inwards).

Be brave! Let your hands go down right to the level of your neck.

Imagine you're holding a stick between your hands. Lift it over your head for one bounce and back, without rearranging your hands.

Do an some inwards Butterflies to get into the rhythm. Then, as the poi come up...

...lift them up over your head so your hands...

...bounce behind you as the poi go down. As the poi come up, lift them...

...back over your head so they bounce in front of you (picture 1).

side view

This is an outwards Butterfly in front and then one behind your head. Each hand moves exactly as it would if it were the outwards hand in a Shoulder Reel, except it is above your head and not over your shoulders - so to prepare for the move, practice doing this with each hand.

You'll need: **Butterfly** (outwards), **Shoulder Reel**.

From an outwards Butterfly, as the poi come up...

...lift them over your head (the backs of your hands face forwards).

Let the poi go down behind you. Your hands turn so palms face upwards.

As the poi come up bring them back over your head, and let them come down in front of you back into an outwards Butterfly (picture 1).

Try to keep your wrists together, so your hands twist but don't come apart or swap positions.

GIANT ANGEL WINGS

This is also known as the 'Giant Butterfly'. The poi do outwards Angel Wings, but do a big circle instead of the Butterfly in front.

You'll need: **Angel Wings** (outwards).

Slow down as you do the big circle.

From outwards Angel Wings...

...bring the poi back over your head from behind you into a big circle...

...cross your arms right over each other at this point in the big circle (your dominant hand should be underneath). Bring the poi up so...

...your poi and hands are in their usual outwards Angel Wings position by the time they get to this point. Now back to picture 1.

Try this with inwards Angel Wings as well. Some people find inwards easier, others find outwards easier.

From an outwards Butterfly, turn 90° to your right into Small Circles in opposite directions. Then turn another 90° to your right into an inwards Butterfly.

You'll need: **Butterfly** (inwards and outwards), **Small Circles**.

Start with an outwards Butterfly. As your poi come up...

...start to turn 90° to your right. Move your right poi as you turn so that it lands on your right side in a forwards circle. Your left poi, which stayed in the same place, is now doing backwards circles. You're now in small circles. When you're ready...

...as your poi come up, start to turn another 90° to your right. Move your left hand as you turn so that it lands on top of (or under) your right hand (which has stayed in the same place) into an inwards Butterfly as the poi come down.

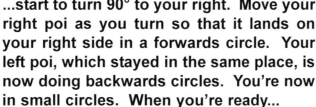

You can also skip pictures 3 & 4, going straight from outwards Butterfly to inwards Butterfly in one beat of the poi without stopping to do Small Circles.

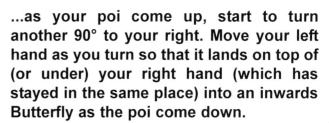

Try the same turn from an inwards Butterfly, turning 90° into Small Circles, and then another 90° into an outwards Butterfly.

MĀORI POI SPINNING

Contemporary poi spinning has its roots in the traditional poi spinning of the Māori culture of New Zealand. The Māori have spun poi for hundreds of years, and still do today. The Māori word 'poi' means several different things - in this context it refers to what you've been spinning for the past few weeks!

Māori poi spinning is a little different to the contemporary poi that takes up most of this book:

The poi the Māori use don't have tails or handles, and are used not only for spinning but also for knocking against your body to make rhythmic sounds.

The Māori most often use one of two types of poi - the 'short' poi and the 'long' poi. Short poi can be anything from about 9 to 25 cm in length, a perfect length for tapping against your body. Long poi are about the length of your arm, and are used much like contemporary poi - but they are also tapped on your body using moves like the Wraps on pages 84 & 85.

Māori poi spinners might spin one, two, three, four or even *five* poi at one time! Now *that's* talent.

Māori poi performances are energetic and visually stunning, and often there's a whole group of highly skilled performers spinning in perfect time with each other. The dance is usually accompanied by a chant or song that tells a story. The performers tap their poi against their bodies, making the percussion to the piece they are dancing to, and at the same time they use their voices, hands, eyes, bodies and feet to help narrate the story of the dance. Their costumes are usually brightly coloured and, to enhance the dancers' movements, they often have long tassels on them, like the skirt shown opposite. Using loads of energy and tapping into their emotions is very important to Māori performers, making their shows brilliant to watch.

These tassels are made of flax. You hold the poi here or by the string just above the tassels.

Cord of flax.

The ball of the poi was made of a bulrush casing, and stuffed with bulrush pith. The casing was often beautifully woven and patterned, and sometimes decorated with shells and awē. Today it is often made of more modern materials.

Some poi have these 'awē' - decorative bunches of hair.

Here are a couple of classic Māori poi moves. The One-Handed Butterfly is often done with two long poi - or even with two in each hand! The tap is more of a short poi move. You'll need: **Butterfly**.

ONE-HANDED BUTTERFLY

If you lay your poi out in a line, handle to handle, you can start this move by grabbing the handles with one hand and whipping the poi up from the ground!

Start with a poi in each hand, but without putting the fingers of your left hand through the handle. Do a Butterfly, and when you're ready take your left poi in your right hand between your middle fingers. Let go with your left hand, and bounce the poi up and down with your right hand to keep the Butterfly going.

Both these moves take a fair bit of practice. They're easier if you use poi without tails.

You need to tilt your hand up and down a bit to stop the poi tangling - just as with the two handed Butterfly.

A POPULAR TAP WITH THE SHORT POI.

THUMP

Spin a backwards circle. As the poi comes up, flick your hand back so the poi taps against your arm. Then go into forwards circles.

When you learn a trick, always spin really **slowly**. This gives you a lot more time to think and to notice what may be going wrong, so you can iron out any problems. And it doesn't hurt so much when you hit yourself! After you've mastered the move, you can go as fast as you like.

Use a **mirror** or some big windows to help you, especially when you first do anything behind your head. It will also let you check that your timing and planes are just right, and will help you spot what might be going wrong if you're having trouble.

Learn every trick in **both directions** - in 'play' and in 'rewind'. With turns learn to turn to your left and to your right. With other moves, learn to do the move clockwise and anticlockwise, or inwards and outwards, or forwards and backwards. Then you'll be able to do the move you want whenever you want to - not only when you are facing a particular way!

Try to make your **planes** as neat as possible. Not only do turns become easier, but your tricks will look loads better.

INTERMEDIATE MOVES

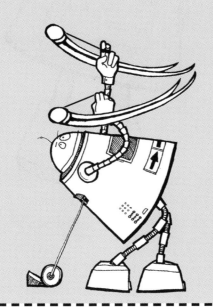

ALTERNATING — OPPOSITE REELS

To get ready for Alternating Reels, have a go at Opposite Reels. The poi spin in opposite directions, so they're both going outwards or both going inwards. The poi both do a circle in front of you and then a circle behind you.
You'll need: **Reels**.

OUTWARDS HIP REELS

When you **alternate** a move, both hands are doing exactly the same sequence of circles, but one hand is always one beat behind the other in the sequence. It's brilliant practice for starting to move your hands independently of each other, so you can eventually put circles with each hand wherever you want them, instead of being limited to particular moves. If you want to invent your own alternating moves, have a look at **places to spin a circle** on pages 71-73.

The poi are the perfect distance apart to tangle - keep them flat and one a little in front of the other.

Both hands do what the outwards hand does in a Reel - an outwards circle in front, and then an outwards circle behind.

Feel free to try an inwards Hip Reel, and try this with Shoulder Reels too.

Your hands do Reels in opposite directions, but one poi is *behind* when the other is *in front* - although they are still in parallel time (they both reach the bottom of their circles at the same time.)

You'll need: **Opposite Reels**.

HIP REELS: OUTWARDS...

... AND INWARDS

SHOULDER REELS: ('MEXICAN WAVE')

To start, get one poi going, and then start the second poi in front of you when the first poi is behind you.

This is easier than the Opposite Reels because you don't tangle as much!

Do outwards Hip Reels, but as the right hand does its circle behind, the left does its circle in front. On the next beat...

...your hands swap. This is also known as the 'Low Wave'.

Let both hands spin inwards Hip Reels, but alternate so one hand is in front when the other is behind.

Spin an outwards Shoulder Reel, but alternate it. You get the idea! It's also known as the 'Mexican Wave'. Try it inwards too.

Make sure you can feel both poi reach the bottom of their circles at the same time, one in front of you and one behind you.

ALTERNATING REEL TURNS

There are loads of turns you can do from Alternating Reels. Here's one example: starting with *inwards* Alternating Reels, you turn 180° letting the poi land in *outwards* Alternating Reels. You begin to turn when the poi are at the bottom of their circles, and finish by the time the poi have reached the bottom again - so you are turning 180° within one beat of the poi.
You'll need: **Alternating Reels**.

Go straight into outwards Alternating Reels from here - bring your right poi in front and your left poi behind you.

Start from an inwards Alternating Reel. When your right poi is in front...

...turn to your right as the poi come up, and...

...keep turning...

...so you have turned 180° by the time the poi land in an outwards Alternating Reel. Your right poi lands behind you.

You could also turn 90° and do a Small Circle (in opposite directions) for one beat before finishing the other 90° of the turn. Or you could turn a full 360° in one beat of the poi, to get you back where you started!

Try a few other Alternating Reel Turns, (there are loads!), a few of which are described below. The aim is to turn within one beat of the poi. If you can do this in a few different ways you'll improve your *general* ability to turn, so you'll be a step closer to inventing turns on the spot as you flow, without having to stick to turns you've already learnt. You'll need: **Alternating Reel Turns**.

Always start to turn as the poi come up, and finish the turn by the time the poi are at the bottom again.

The turn shown above is the same as the turn on the previous page, except the right hand ends up *in front* as the turn finishes. Every time you do an Alternating Reel Turn, you can choose which hand should end up in front of you when you *finish* the turn. You can also choose which hand is in front of you when you *start* the turn - so you could start when your left is in front (instead of your right hand as shown here).

You can also turn to your left instead of your right. That's a lot of variations - eight in total! Of course, you have these same eight options when you start from outwards circles (instead of inwards circles as shown here).

Lastly you can do all of these by your shoulders (instead of your hips) - giving you a whopping 32 variations!

THE SWEEP

This is the Mexican Wave (outwards Alternating Shoulder Reels), with big circles in front instead of small ones. Ease yourself into it by doing the Mexican Wave, and start to make the circles in front bigger and bigger until they are huge. The circles behind stay the same.

You'll need: **Alternating Reels** (Mexican Wave).

Big circles take longer than small circles, so find a happy medium.

Start from the Mexican Wave, and as a poi comes over your head from behind you, reach it up, down ...

...and around in a big circle, reaching right across your body as the poi comes up. (The other poi spins the circle behind you.)

Then let it do a small circle behind your head as the other hand does the big circle.

If you prefer spinning inwards, try this spinning inwards too.

The great thing about alternating is that your body isn't in a symmetrical position at any one time, so you can move your body asymmetrically to vary the trace drawn by the tails. This also lets you dance a bit more!

Using the Sweep as an example:

This is the fire trace one poi makes in the sweep - an outwards circle behind your shoulder and a big circle in front.

This is the fire trace one poi makes if you reach really high as each poi comes up behind you.

This is the fire trace one poi makes if, as each poi comes down from over your head, you lean towards it and turn your body slightly towards it. You could even step towards it a bit. Let your body move rhythmically with the poi.

Try some of your own variations in body motion with this and other alternating moves you learn.

AN EXTENDED REEL

This is an extension of the Reel, and is a more complicated move to alternate. (The alternated version is the Wiggle on the next page.) Both poi do a circle behind the shoulder, a circle behind your hip, and then carry up to the shoulder again. The poi spin outwards in parallel time.

You'll need: **Opposite Reels**, **Linking Reels**.

It helps to shrug your shoulders forwards here.

Carry both poi up to Shoulder Reel level (crossing your arms as you bring them up) and let the poi fall behind in a shoulder circle.

As the poi come down, push your palms out a little and bring the poi down...

...into hip circles behind you.

As the poi come down, start to bring them in front of you again. Now back to picture 1.

To do the move inwards, reverse the sequence of circles, so you spin *hip-shoulder-carry* instead of *carry-shoulder-hip*. This is the move in 'rewind'.

Now alternate the Extended Reel: One hand always stays one beat ahead of the other. It's tricky at first getting your hands to do different things, but it's worth the effort: it's a step on the way to being able to spontaneously put circles wherever you want to with each hand while you spin, so you won't always need to stick to set moves.

You'll need: **Extended Reel.**

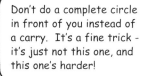

Don't do a complete circle in front of you instead of a carry. It's a fine trick - it's just not this one, and this one's harder!

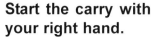

Each hand does *carry- shoulder-hip* just like in the Extended Reel. The poi spin outwards.

Start the carry with your right hand.

As your right hand does the shoulder circle, start the carry with your left hand.

As your right hand does the hip circle, your left hand does the shoulder circle.

As your right hand does the carry, your left does the hip circle. Now back to the middle picture.

Try putting some body movement (page 67) of your own in this move, to make it more expressive or more fun!

THE INWARDS WIGGLE

This is the Wiggle in 'rewind' (page 17). To rewind a move, not only does the direction change (in this case from outwards Wiggle to inwards Wiggle), but the sequence of circles that each hand does is reversed - now it is *carry-hip-shoulder* instead of *shoulder-hip-carry*. Again the beats alternate, so one hand is always one beat behind the other. You'll need: **Extended Reel** (inwards).

Spinning the poi inwards, get each hand to do the sequence on its own first: *carry-hip- shoulder*.

Start the carry with your right hand - it is now the leading hand.

As your lead hand starts the hip circle, start the carry with your other hand.

As your lead hand starts the shoulder circle, start the hip circle with your other hand.

As your lead hand does the carry, your other hand does the shoulder circle. Now back to the middle picture.

You might prefer this to the Wiggle if you enjoy inwards moves more than outwards ones.

To invent your own moves, a good start is to play with all the places you can put a circle. A few places to do a circle in the wall plane are shown here. Have a spin with each arm, finding lots of places to do a circle and working out how to link them, experimenting with both inwards and outwards.

You can do a big circle, and little circles anywhere along its edge.

You can also fill the big circle with smaller ones - like in the place where Reels are...

...or along your body line like where Butterflies are.

There are loads of other places to do a circle (like through your legs), so don't limit yourself to what's shown here. Also, have a play in the side planes.

You can do all the circles either behind or in front of you (except you can't do the big circle behind you unless you're double jointed!), and either inwards or outwards.

DIFFERENT WAYS TO SPIN THE SAME CIRCLE

Most circles in a particular place can be done in a couple of ways. For example, any circle that involves you reaching across your body can be done with your arm reaching either across the front of your body or behind your body. When you play with the places you can put a circle, have a go at doing different circles in different ways.

This circle can be spun by reaching across the front of your body...

...or behind.

Here's another one that can be done reaching in front...

This one takes a lot of practice. You use it for the Behind The Back Waist Wrap.

...or behind (Ow!)

This also works with circles by your shoulder or in front of your legs, and with circles that cross your body in the side planes.

You can invent moves by playing with putting circles in different places - because let's face it, putting circles in places is what poi spinning is all about. So you could go on inventing forever: sometimes you can get a stonkingly nice move - other times it just won't work, usually because your arms are attached to your body at the shoulder. Here are some ideas for inventing in this way:

Choose a sequence of circles with one hand. Now mirror those circles with the other hand at the same time, to get a new trick in opposite directions in parallel time. Then you could try alternating your new trick, (page 62) making sure one hand is always a beat behind the other, to get...another new trick! Tricks with up to three beats (four at a stretch) are usually okay to alternate - more than that and it becomes rare that the move is even possible, or else it's madly complicated.

Another idea is to spin a sequence of circles with your hands held together so the poi spin as one poi, strings almost touching, in parallel time. You can really flow with this one - try turning and putting the poi in odd places, and turning whilst leaving your poi where they were. It takes some practice to do this without tangling. Next, you could work out how to do the whole parallel time sequence in split time. Work out which hand leads (which hand is half a circle in front) and which hand is on top at each point by trial and error.

You could try spinning a circle with one poi, and finding somewhere to spin the other poi at the same time. Move both poi to new locations as often as you like. This can be done in parallel time, split time, same direction or opposite directions.

For even more ideas, look at the section on Push-Thrus and Take-Outs overleaf.

Link your circles using carries (page 13) - even very small carries - or matching points (page 24). Some circles can't be linked together directly: For example, an *outwards* circle behind your hip can't be linked directly to an outwards circle behind your shoulder because your arm just won't twist that way. You need to carry the poi in front of your body.

INWARDS PUSH-THRU

Push-Thrus are based on the Butterfly, but to do them you need to be able to do the Butterfly with either hand on top - instead of always with your dominant hand on top. This also allows you to invent moves based on Take-Outs, where you take a poi out of the Butterfly to spin circles in other places.

Also known as 'Thread the Needle'. When you do it well, it looks as though the two circles traced by the poi tails are moving impossibly through each other. The poi spin inwards, and your hands push forwards and back, swapping on every beat. First, you need to be able to do the inwards Butterfly with either hand on top, so go back to page 52 and teach yourself the Butterfly again, this time with your non-dominant hand on top.

You'll need: **Butterfly** (inwards).

STEP ONE

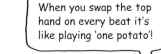

When you swap the top hand on every beat it's like playing 'one potato'!

So, you can do an inwards Butterfly with either hand on top. Now do a few inwards Butterflies with your right hand on top, and...

...as the poi come up move your left hand up, so...

...it lands on top of the other hand into a Butterfly as the poi reach the bottom. Practice until you can swap hands every beat.

STEP TWO

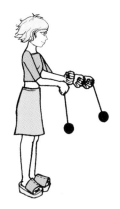

Next, whilst still swapping the top hand on every beat, every time a hand lands on the other push it fowards a bit, and pull the bottom hand back a bit.

STEP THREE: THE PUSH-THRU

Now all you have to do is exaggerate the movement: As you bring a hand back from being underneath, bring it right back to land on your shoulder...

...let it slide down your arm (as you pull the other arm back to your shoulder) and...

...extend it in a good punch! Keep doing this on every beat, and...smile!

Slide your hand along your arm for the best effect, because then both circles share the same central line.

OUTWARDS PUSH-THRU

This is the inwards Push-Thru in 'rewind'. It's the same except your poi spin outwards, and you move your hands *under* each other, bringing your hand back into your armpit and sliding forwards under the other arm. First make sure you can do outwards Butterflies with *either* hand underneath (page 53).

You'll need: **Butterfly** (outwards).

STEP ONE   **STEP TWO**   **STEP THREE**

So, you can now spin a Butterfly with either hand underneath. Next, start from an outwards Butterfly with your right hand underneath...	...and as the poi go down bring your left hand down so that...	...it lands under your right hand into a Butterfly when the poi are at the bottom. Now do the same to bring your right hand down.	When you can swap hands every beat, slip each hand forwards a bit as it lands underneath, and bring the other hand back a bit.	Exaggerate this motion: bring your hand back to your other armpit, and then slide it forwards under the other arm.

From a Butterfly or Push-Thru, take one hand *out* of the Butterfly and let it spin a circle anywhere for one beat, keeping the poi in parallel time. Then bring it back into the Butterfly. Next, let the other hand try the same thing. Check out Places to Spin a Circle (page 71) for some ideas. You'll need: **Push-Thrus**.

> You can do a Butterfly with either hand on top, so you can choose to take a poi from the bottom or from the top of the Butterfly, and bring it back to the top or bottom.

> Yeah, sometimes it's easier to bring your hand back to the top (like from some shoulder circles) and sometimes to the bottom.

The hand that is not doing the Take-Out stays where it is, doing the Butterfly. Sometimes it takes more concentration to keep this hand in the same place than to move the other hand!

TAKE-OUT SEQUENCES

You can use Take-Out sequences to invent some unusual tricks. First, start with a Butterfly and then take a hand out and do *a few* circles in different places before bringing the hand back to the Butterfly. This is a Take-Out sequence. Find a sequence you like, and make sure each hand can do it. Next, let one hand do the sequence, bring it back for one beat of the Butterfly, and then let the other hand do the sequence. When you invent moves in this way, you'll need to work out if it's easier to bring your hand back from the Take-Out sequence to the top or the bottom of the Butterfly. If you need to bring your hand back to the bottom, the sequence should start with the hand on top.

You'll need: **Take-Outs**.

When you're comfortable with this, skip the Butterfly and take one hand out to do the sequence as the other hand is coming back from doing it - see page 79.

Instead of keeping the hand that's doing Butterflies in one place, you could see what other circles it can do that fit the Take-Out sequence of the other hand.

The shoulder circles are both behind your body.

This is a nicely tangleful Take-Out sequence. Each hand spins this sequence: *Butterfly - Butterfly - far shoulder - same shoulder*. The poi spin outwards in parallel time, and the hands *don't* meet in a butterfly in between sequences - one hand starts the Take-Outs as the other hand returns to the Butterfly place.

You'll need: **Push-Thrus** (outwards).

Get each hand on its own first, spinning Butterfly - *Butterfly - far shoulder - same shoulder*. Spin outwards. If you try it you'll find that there are two *beats* in the Butterfly position, but only one full Butterfly *circle*.

Start from a Butterfly. As the right poi comes up, take it out to do the far shoulder circle.

Your right hand then does the near shoulder circle whilst your left hand does a Butterfly.

As the left poi goes up, take it to the far shoulder. As the right poi goes down, bring it to the Butterfly place.

Your left poi does a near shoulder circle whilst your right poi does a Butterfly. Now back to picture 1.

First, try the trick with a few Butterflies between each hand doing the sequence. Then do fewer and fewer Butterflies in between until there are none.

When you do a few in a row, it feels like one hand does the two shoulder circles whilst the other does two Butterfly beats. Then your hands swap jobs.

PIROUETTES

To spin a Pirouette you turn 360° by the time the poi complete one circle.

PARALLEL PIROUETTE

You turn 360° in the time it takes the poi to spin one Big Circle in parallel time.

You'll need: **Big Circle** (parallel time).

Start from a Big Circle. As the poi go past your feet, start to turn, so that...

...by the time the poi are at the top of the circle, you have turned 180°. Keep turning, so that...

...you are back where you started as the poi pass your feet again (picture 1).

Turn the same way the poi go past your feet - if they go from left to right, turn to your right.

For this one keep your hands half a circle apart. Try starting from a Giant Windmill (page 33). This time, follow your lead hand: you want to start the turn as your lead hand passes your legs, and to have turned a full circle by the time it passes your legs again.

You'll need: **Giant Windmill**, **Pirouette**.

And...stretch!

Try as much as possible to keep your arms exactly half a circle apart the whole time - and slow down as much as you can.

OPPOSITE PIROUETTE

You turn a full 360°, but this time one poi is spinning a big backwards circle, and the other is spinning a big forwards circle. The turn feels very fast - it's worth trying it with two sticks first to get the feel of it, and then trying it in small stages with poi.

You'll need: **Big Circle** (opposite directions), **Pirouette**.

0° / 360°
Your hands
are down.

90°
Your hands
are out
horizontally.

180°
Your
hands are
up.

270°
Your hands
are out
horizontally.

Start from Big Circles in opposite directions, or with your hands by your sides. As the poi come up...

...turn towards the hand spinning forwards, so that by the time the poi are at the top...

...you've turned a full 180°. As the poi come down...

...turn another 90°. By the time the poi are at the bottom you are back at the first picture, with the poi on either side of you.

You can turn just 90°, or 180° or 270°, if you just use a few of the stages above. You can start the turn at any of the stages.

For an extra challenge, try doing a few of these continuously. Then try to walk in a straight line!

Being able to stop your poi in a stylish way (and not by accident) is a landmark point in the journey of a poister. Stops are brilliant moments of drama, letting you add descriptive gestures and a surprise change of tempo to your otherwise flowing spinning.

Stopping *both* your poi also lets you change direction, so you can go from inwards to outwards or forwards to backwards without turning around - useful if you don't fancy having your back to your audience half the time. If you stop only *one* poi, and then start it going again the other way, you can link tricks where your poi are both going in the same direction to tricks where they are going in opposite directions. At last.

Stops are split into '**bounces**' (where you knock the poi on something - yourself, the floor, a passer by...) and '**stills**' (where the poi are stopped in mid air without making contact with anything - these are much safer.) On the next few pages are my favourite stops.

To master a stop, practice the stop with each arm on its own and then with both together. You'll need to adjust the length of your poi to get some of the stops right.

Next, try getting both hands to do the stop in the middle of a trick. Mess about with tricks that are in parallel time, split time, same direction, opposite directions, the wall planes and the side planes. Now that'll keep you busy.

Finally, have a play with stopping just one poi whilst keeping the other going: pick a trick where the poi go in the same direction and link it to a trick where the poi go in opposite directions by stopping just one poi.

You can also have a go at doing different kinds of stops with each hand. It's *guaranteed* to improve your co-ordination!

From forwards circles the poi wraps around your arm and bounces off into backwards circles. How many times it wraps around your arm and where on your arm it bounces depends on the length of the poi.
You'll need: **Small Circles, Stops**.

> If the poi gets stuck between your upper and lower arm, adjust the length.

> Wraps are easier at first if your poi are going very fast, so they really bounce off.

THUMP

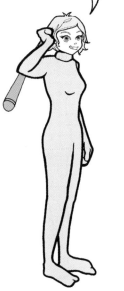

THUMP

Spin a forwards circle. As the poi comes down, stick your hand into your armpit, and your elbow out to the side at shoulder height.

You may need to help the poi unwrap by drawing some circles with your elbow, shrugging the poi off, and then *pull* it back into orbit.

The poi will wrap round your upper and lower arm, and the head will bounce off your arm so the poi unwraps into backwards circles.

From a backwards circle put your hand on your shoulder as the poi is descending, and stick your elbow out at shoulder height.

You'll need to point your fingers towards your elbow so the poi wraps around both your upper and lower arm. If the poi wraps on the other side of your hand (around your shoulder) you won't be able to unwrap it.

The poi will wrap around your upper and lower arm, and then bounce off and unwrap into forwards circles.

This is another Wrap Stop, but you only let the poi wrap a bit before you *slap* it!

THUMP

The poi wrap only half the way round a limb, and bounce off. You can do this on any part of your body, someone else, tall chairs, drainpipes...
You'll need: **Small Circles**, **Stops**.

BOF

Spin some backwards circles. As the poi comes up stick your elbow out and put your hand above your upper arm, palm open.

Slap your poi soundly to send it into forwards circles.

If you spin slowly you can bring your hand down towards your poi as you slap it, so you don't miss!

Spin a circle and put a body part in the way. Make sure your hand is not too close to the part, or your poi will wrap all the way round and probably get stuck. When the poi has bounced off, pull it back the way it came.

If you put your hand in the way of the string, you can let the poi wrap completely around your hand to end a show.

85

KICKS

You spin your poi. You kick it. It spins off in the other direction (hopefully). Wear shoes so that you don't hurt your feet. You'll need: **Small Circles, Stops**.

Just make sure you look up, not to the side. If you miss your foot and hit your leg, fake it - people don't usually notice!

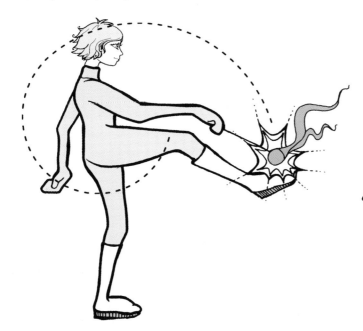

From forwards circles you can kick your poi. You need to help it bounce off into the right plane by controlling it with your hand - or it might fly off in any direction! Or, you can just tap it gently with your foot but pull it hard with your hand so it looks like you kicked it hard - but a good *kick* is definitely more satisfying!

Some people say that the poi keeps in plane better when you let it bounce off the sole of your foot, rather than kicking it with the top of your foot.

This one's is easier than it looks, and it looks pretty fab! Spin backwards circles. As the poi comes up start to reach way over your head, look up at the sky, and kick your leg up backwards. After a few tries you'll be able to line your poi and foot up more often than not.

Kicks are easier once you've learnt the Basic Still on the opposite page. Then you can slow your poi and kick it when it's still, so you have time to aim your foot.

THE BASIC STILL

Don't let the string sag at any point!

The poi stops suspended in the air for just an instant, as if it was a rigid stick. It's then pulled back the way it came.

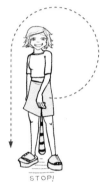

THE END STOP

THE PUSH STOP

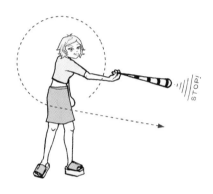

Spin an inwards circle. As the poi gets to the top of its circle...

...move your hand very slightly towards the poi to slacken the tension on the string. Slow down a lot, and keep the string slack by moving your hand a little with the poi as it continues its circle. The poi will be spinning in a slightly larger circle now that the tension is reduced.

At the point where you want the poi to leave the circle push your fingers a tiny bit in the direction you want the poi to go, and then stop your hand. The poi will pause in mid air for an instant. Then, just before the head of the poi starts to fall, pull the poi into an outwards circle.

From an inwards circle do a Basic Still but slacken the tension a little earlier. Then push your hand down whilst slowing down - to take all the momentum out of the poi. The poi should stop, motionless, a couple of inches above the floor- a good way to end a piece!

From an outwards circle slacken the tension as the poi goes down. As it reaches the bottom of its circle push it with your hand as far as you can to one side, (whilst slowing down), so the head of the poi travels in a straight line. Just before the head of the poi falls, pull the poi back the way it came.

THE BUTTERFLY STOP

Here's one tasty stop that I really like. Otherwise it's up to you to come up with some great moves that use stops.
You'll need: **Butterfly, Basic Still.**

Hold the Still as long as possible without the poi drooping.

Your left poi does a circle and a half (at least) between the last picture and this one.

Do an inwards Butterfly. As the poi come up, bring your left poi up a bit, slow it down, and let it do a Basic Still over your right arm - behind your right poi. Your right poi keeps spinning.

Your left poi comes back to the Butterfly position spinning outwards. As your right poi comes up, let it slow a bit and do a Basic Still the same way your left poi just did. Keep your left hand spinning outwards circles.

Bring your right poi up and out to join your left hand in an outwards Butterfly when it gets to the bottom of its circle.

Club swinging uses two rigid clubs, one held in each hand, swung in similar patterns to those you are doing with poi. It's been around for a long time: heavy wooden clubs were used by Greek athletes in the days of the Greek Empire, and by the Indian military for a few centuries as a form of exercise. More recently, club swinging has been a discipline of rhythmic gymnastics. Contemporary club swinging as a circus art became popular in the 1980s, and some contemporary poi spinning moves are based on established club swinging moves - like the Waist Wrap (page 96).

If you're thinking of taking up club swinging, you'll have the advantage that you know a lot of the moves and are used to spinning circles. However, in the beginning club swinging can be tricky because you have to learn a variety of grips (ways of holding the club) and be able to interchange between them smoothly. Club swinging also requires *even more* wrist flexibility than poi spinning. The advantages when learning club swinging are that you can go as slow as you like - even stop at points to check you are doing it right - and so you don't hit yourself nearly as much (or get tangled!)

Poi spinning and club swinging are very similar and influence each other a lot, but of course there are differences. Many moves are easier to do with clubs than with poi - for example clubs can be stopped in any position for a long time, whilst poi can only be stopped for an instant, and only in some positions (you can't stop your poi when it's pointing upwards). It's also easier to throw and catch clubs than poi, and a blend of club juggling and club swinging has become a beautiful part of some juggling routines. It was also thought that the 'Snake', a popular club swinging move in which the club is manouvered around the arm in which it is held, was not possible with poi. The good news is it *can* be done with poi but with a far greater amount of jiggery pokery to keep the poi looking rigid.

On the other hand, there are lots of things you can do with poi because of the flexible string - like wrapping the poi around a limb, or nudging the string to get various effects. These are all completely impossible with clubs!

If you're interested in learning club swinging check out 'some useful resources' on page 141 for some guides to the art.

Personal style includes many aspects of spinning, from the tricks you choose to do, to the way you move your body and your poi. It's what you choose to do *and* the way you do it - a bit like having an individual dance style. One of the best things about having a personal style is that no one will ever spin the way you do! Also, when people have different styles to each other they begin to invent different things, and so have more to teach each other.

Developing your spinning style takes time. It's easiest when you're on your own and can focus - but don't let doing it in public scare you after the first few times! And you don't need to stick to just one style: you could develop different styles for different moods you might be in, or for different characters that you want to play.

DEVELOPING YOUR OWN TRADEMARK MOVES

It's nice to have moves that no one else is doing, or an aspect of poi spinning that you've developed more than anyone else. You don't need to do every trick there is - just do ones you like, and explore from there.

Sometimes, it works best to just get lost in the flow of your spinning - so you are spinning without thinking or planning - and new moves will just happen as if by magic. In mid flow, you could also try forcing your hands to an unexpected position, and see if that gives you any ideas. Another option is to picture in your head a pattern you want the poi to make, and then pick up your poi and see if you can spin that pattern. Or you could think about how you would like to move your body and your hands in a gesture or a dance move, and then work out how to fit the poi into this.

Also, try choosing an aspect of spinning you are interested in and exploring it. For example, if you are interested in mixing planes (page 94), you could try to invent new moves of that type. Or if you are interested in timing, see if you can find timings other than parallel time and split time to play with.

Another way to get yourself doing new moves is to take any aspect of your poi spinning and change it: the poi you use; the speed you spin at; whether you move around or stay still; whether you keep your arms far from or close to your body; what music you listen to. The list is endless, but find some features and try changing them - you'll get a whole bunch of ideas for new moves.

Every time you learn a new trick, play with it to see if there's anything you can add or vary. And whenever you make a mistake, think about whether it might work as a trick. Lots of mistakes are useless - but some turn out to be real gems - or whole new areas to explore. Stops, for example, could have come from hitting yourself!

DEVELOPING THE WAY YOU DO WHAT YOU DO

This will happen on its own if you spin a lot, but here's a few ideas if you don't know where to start:

Try relaxing before you spin. Anything that helps you clear your head is fine - meditation, yoga, stretching, a quiet coffee. Also, try visualizing how you'd like to feel or look when you spin. This will give you lots of ideas, and build the personality of your poi style.

Another idea is to play some music that you emotionally connect with (or that just makes you want to dance!) and give yourself a long stretch of time to try to connect your poi spinning with the music. At first, you might feel a little stilted, like you can't flow as much as you want to or you can't quite find the way you'd like to spin, but persevere. Your style will start to develop after a few weeks. It'll keep changing and developing as you have new ideas.

It's also useful to tap into your emotional state. If you're feeling shy, angry, happy, playful or sad, try showing it in the way you spin. You can use your spinning to reflect your mood or to put you in a particular mood - many people spin as a kind of meditation, to get them into a peaceful frame of mind.

If you have a picture in your head of how you want your style to look, work on it. Whether you want your style to mimic a particular art (like classical ballet, kung fu or clowning), or a particular character or animal (like a fairy, a daemon, or a cat), or you have some other less definable idea, play at being that character whilst spinning. Think about how your character moves, what gestures it makes and how it feels. A mirror will also help you achieve the look you want.

Finally, you could try some sort of movement course, like dance, mime, acting, yoga or martial arts. Anything that trains your movement will enhance your style.

The best poi spinning is the spinning that *you* like to do most. So there.

THE HORIZONTAL PLANE

Most tricks can be done in a horizontal plane quite easily - except turns or moves that go around your body like the Waist Wrap. You get into the horizontal plane from the vertical plane by gradually changing the plane of your poi, a little bit every beat. Eventually you'll be able to go from one plane to another in just one beat. Here's a few examples:

Loads of the tricks you do can be done in the **horizontal plane,** and of course in an infinite number of diagonal planes. You can also get great effects by **mixing two planes -** so that one poi spins in one plane and the other poi spins in another plane.

HORIZONTAL PIROUETTE

This is easy - and so is the Parallel Pirouette. Opposite Pirouettes won't work in the horizontal plane though.

PUSH-THRU

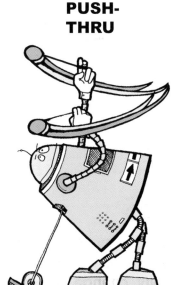

Feel free to try some horizontal Take-Outs.

THE CORKSCREW

Your wrists do need to move a little differently because of the change in plane, but you'll soon get used to it.

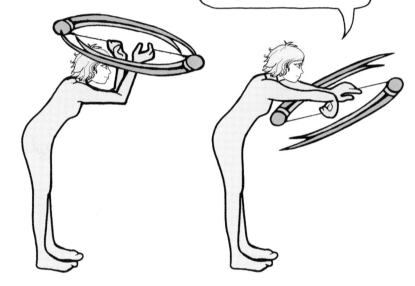

This is a Windmill in the horizontal plane. Start from a Windmill, and bending your upper body forwards slowly change the plane of the poi, holding your hands far from your body as the poi come under your head, and pointing in towards your body.

Of course, you can do horizontal circles anywhere you like - try over and under your arm, your leg and behind your back.

OVERHEAD BUTTERFLY

Do a normal Butterfly and then gradually bend the planes of both poi so you end up doing it over your head.

Other tricks can also be done on a diagonal plane, like the Buzzsaw (page 103) and Pirouettes (page 80).

JUMPING BUTTERFLY

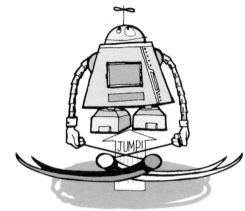

Start from an Overhead Butterfly. As the poi spin towards each other, bring the poi down and jump as they cross under your feet. Keep the strings pointing *diagonally* downwards.

These tricks look very unusual and they frame your body nicely - although they can be a little tangleful at first. Start with the poi in the same plane, and slowly bend the plane of one (or both) poi. It doesn't matter if you spin inwards or outwards, but keep the poi in parallel time all the time.

You'll need: **Overhead Butterfly**, **Behind Your Back Butterfly**.

SATELLITE

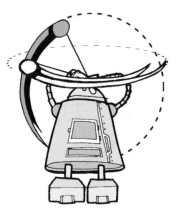

Start from an Overhead Butterfly (page 93). Every beat, tilt the plane of the poi in the back hand a little until it is behind you in the wall plane, whilst your other poi is still horizontal. Keep your wrists touching, and just over the back of your head.

ANOTHER SATELLITE

Start from a Butterfly behind you. Bend over. Then every beat tilt the plane of the poi in your upper hand a little, keeping the poi in parallel time, until the poi (in this case the white poi) in your upper hand (the hand visible in the picture) is spinning in the horizontal plane over your back. The poi in your lower hand is still spinning behind you in the wall plane. Your wrists should still be touching, and positioned just over the base of your spine.

THE ATOM

From an Overhead Butterfly, slowly bend the planes of both poi so they are spinning diagonally in parallel time. Try to keep your wrists touching. Your wrists stay in the same spot just above your head.

THE WAIST WRAP

THE HIPMILL

The Hipmill is step one of the Waist Wrap. It is similar to the Windmill, but by one hip. The poi spin in the same direction in split time, spinning one circle in front and one circle behind the left hip. The left hand leads (it's the first hand to come in front and the first hand to go behind).
You'll need: **Windmill**, **Small Circles** (split time).

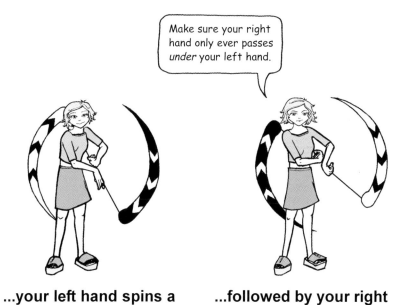

Make sure your right hand only ever passes *under* your left hand.

Keeping in split time, your left hand spins an outwards circle in front of your left hip...

...followed by your right hand (which spins inwards). Then...

...your left hand spins a circle behind your hip...

...followed by your right hand. Then your left poi comes in front of you again (picture 1).

An easy way to get into the Hipmill is to spin the circles in parallel time first (as if the poi were one poi). Then split the poi into split time, with your left hand leading.

THE WAIST WRAP

This is a classic club swinging move (see page 89). Starting just like the Hipmill, the poi spin a circle behind your left hip, then a circle in front of your belly button, then a circle behind your right hip, and then carry up over your head to behind your left hip again - so there are three circles and a carry in all. The poi spin in split time in the same direction.

You'll need: **Hipmill, Weave Turn** (from forwards).

Start as with the Hipmill, doing a circle behind your left hip in split time. Your left hand leads.

As your left hand comes in front and you start to do the circle in front of your hip...

...bring your hands to the middle of your body and let them uncross...

...and recross, just like in the Non-Turning Weave Turn from forwards. As your hands recross...

You can link the Waist Wrap to the Weaves using matching points (page 24).

Only make one circle here with each hand or you'll end up in a Backwards Weave. As soon as your left hand comes up behind you, go straight into the carry.

...let your left hand reach around to do a circle behind your right hip...

...followed by your right hand. As soon as your left hand has done one circle behind your right hip, carry it up...

...followed by your right hand, all the way round...

...to the first circle - a circle behind your left hip. Now back to picture 1.

Slow down for the carry, and stretch your arms as much as you can. Keep your hands half a circle apart - don't let your right hand catch up with your left.

Try doing the whole Waist Wrap with your wrists touching (except for the carry) for maximum neatness.

THE GIANT WAIST WRAP

The circle that you do in front of your belly button in the Waist Wrap can be made into a big circle if you stretch out your arms and slow down. It gives a nice effect, and is a great place to do 'Lock Outs', explained on the next few pages.

You'll need: **Waist Wrap**.

Do the first circle of the Waist Wrap. As your arms come in front of your belly button and uncross (to do the second circle)...

...stretch your arms out to do a big slow circle in follow time...

...and as your arms recross, carry on with the Waist Wrap (the circle behind your right hip).

A Lock Out is when in the middle of a big circle you lock your arms in position (when your hands are far apart) so the poi spin a quick small circle. You then continue with the big circle. It's easy, and it's a lovely flourish. First, try one in a Giant Weave. You'll need: **Giant Weave**.

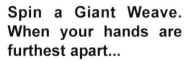

Spin a Giant Weave. When your hands are furthest apart...

...*stop* your arms with a jolt. The poi will each start to spin a small circle in split time, on your right. These are the Lock Outs.

Follow the path of the poi with your fingers, but keep your arms still. As the poi get to the bottom, scoop them up...

...to carry on where you left off in the big circle.

You can do the same thing in a Giant Backwards Weave.

If your poi collide, get one to spin a little in front of the other as you do the Lock Out - so the black poi conceals the white poi in picture 2 or vice versa. Also try stretching your hands really far apart.

99

LOCK OUT SEQUENCES

You can do more than one Lock Out in a big circle - shown here in the Waist Wrap. In fact you can do as many as you like. Each time you finish a Lock Out, use a carry to get to the next Lock Out or to finish the circle. The poi don't change direction, so you can only link to a Lock Out further along in the big circle you are spinning.
You'll need: **Giant Waist Wrap**, **Lock Outs**.

Do a Giant Waist Wrap.

This is almost the first point in the big circle where you can do a Lock Out comfortably. Then carry...

...to do another Lock Out, and carry...

...to do another Lock Out. This is almost the last place you can do a Lock Out easily. Then...

...continue with the Giant Waist Wrap.

Only a few places to do Lock Outs are shown here - for example you can also do them with your arms held diagonally.

You can also put Lock Outs in other big circles - for example in the Giant Windmill, the Hipmill, and the Weave Turns.

Try Lock Outs in big circles in opposite directions. Above your head and by your feet the poi make circles that overlap, but elsewhere the poi are various distances apart. You'll need: **Big Circle** (opposite), **Giant Angel Wings**.

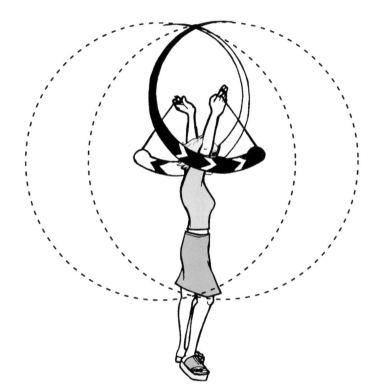

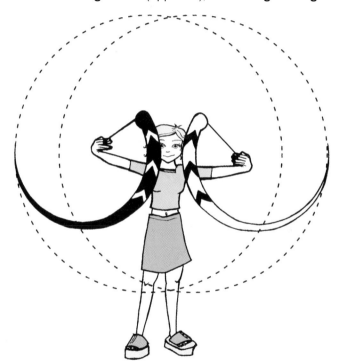

Do a Big Circle in opposite directions, and put Lock Outs in it. Try when both your hands are at the top, both at the bottom, or one stretching in front and one behind.

You can also put Lock Outs in big circles in the wall plane - in Giant Angel Wings for example.

For a technical challenge, try doing Lock Outs continuously whilst doing a Pirouette.

CHANGING LENGTH IN MID-SPIN

Some tricks need long poi and others need short poi, so it's useful to be able to change the length of your poi as you spin, by letting them wrap around your hands. This is especially useful for the Buzzsaw and for spinning a poi Through Your Legs.

You'll need: **Small Circles**.

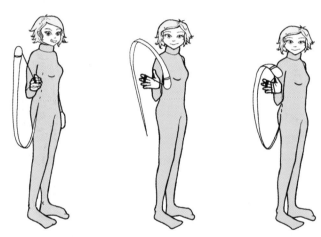

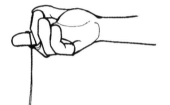

From any circle, (for example a forwards circle), open your hand, put it in the path of your poi string, and let the poi wrap around your palm to get the length you want.

When the poi are the length you want, you can catch them so the string falls between your first and second fingers, and hangs from the back of your hand as usual. Or, you can catch the string between your fingers and thumb as shown on the opposite page.

It's quite nice to play with wrapping and unwrapping the string in the middle of the Weave.

To get the poi to unwrap again, spin the poi on the other side of your body and it will unwrap if you let it.

You can let the poi wrap completely around your hands to stop them.

You spin very short poi in follow time in a flat circle between your arms. Also known as the 'Wheel', (because it looks like one), this move needs poi short enough so you don't hit your face, and a different way of holding the poi.

You'll need: **Small Circles** (follow time), **Changing Length in Mid-Spin**.

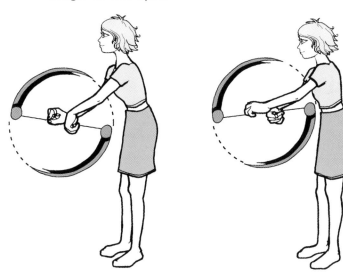

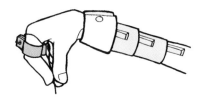

If you hold your poi with the string between your thumb and fingers, you can point the poi where you want it to go. This grip is also useful for spinning the poi Through Your Legs.

A popular trick is to take the Buzzsaw through your legs whilst you do a forwards roll. Very flashy, but difficult and a little dangerous: You need to keep your hands off the floor the whole time, which means landing on your neck if you're not careful. You need to be flexible (and very warmed up) and practice on a crash mat without poi first - but you're accepting the risk of injury if you try this. To minimise the risk, get a little training from a gymnastics or tumbling coach. It sounds a bit melodramatic, but hurting your neck can be serious. You have been warned!

Keeping the poi in follow time, let them chase each other round the edge of a circle, passing in between your arms.

You can also try the Buzzsaw with the poi spinning in opposite directions - change directions by tapping a poi against your body.

THROUGH YOUR LEGS

This is easier than it looks! Practice each hand on its own until you can do circles through your legs inwards, outwards, forwards and backwards. It helps if you have short poi, and use the Buzzsaw grip. Then put these circles into moves you can already do. On the next pages are examples in parallel and split time, and opposite directions. You'll need: **Small Circles**, **Inwards and Outwards Circles**, **Changing Length in Mid-Spin**, **Buzzsaw**.

FROM IN FRONT

Start with a circle in front of you in the wall plane. When the poi is at the bottom of its circle, take it through your legs to spin a circle behind you.

As the poi goes down in front of you, bend your upper body down (this will help you reach through your legs in just a minute...) but keep your hand high enough so the poi doesn't hit the floor. Slow the poi down. At its lowest point, point the poi through your legs. Reach through your legs a split second after the poi has gone through, and give the poi a good flick to make the circle behind you. It helps if you come up onto your toes as the poi go through your legs. At its lowest point bring the poi back through your legs to spin a circle in front of you again.

The poi doesn't need to make a full sized circle - you can slant the string so the circle through your legs is a little smaller than usual, (this might stop you hitting yourself,) but a full sized circle is the ideal.

FROM BEHIND

Spin an outwards circle behind you, then take it through your legs to spin in front of you. This works the same way as from in front, But lean your body back and towards the arm going through your legs.

FROM THE SIDE PLANE

Through the legs is easier with shorter poi.

Spin a circle next to you in the side plane, then take it through your legs to spin a circle on the other side of your body. All the tips that apply to 'From in Front' apply here. Not too hard, is it?

BUTTERFLY

This is quite a tough one. Think of it as upside down Angel Wings: your hands don't move apart but stay together in the same relative position, so the hand that is on top in front of you is underneath behind you, and the poi in this hand is in front when the poi are at the top.
You'll need: **Angel Wings**.

Start with a Butterfly in front of you. As the poi go down, bend over (a lot!), and take the poi through your legs at the lowest point. Do a Butterfly and bring the poi back in front.

THROUGH YOUR LEGS HIP REEL

This is the same as the Hip Reel, except when the poi do the circle behind you, one poi gets behind by going through your legs. Here I've shown the outwards hand going through - but try it with the inwards hand going through instead.
You'll need: **Hip Reel.**

Start doing a Hip Reel, your legs wide apart. As the poi go down take your left poi through your legs. Your right poi goes diagonally past your legs as usual.

Your left poi does a circle through your legs whilst your right poi does a circle behind you.

When your poi are at the bottom of their circles, pull your left poi back through your legs, and let both poi do a circle in front of you as in the Hip Reel.

THROUGH YOUR LEGS WAIST WRAP

This is one way to go through your legs in split time. As you finish the circle in front of your belly button in the Waist Wrap, you take the poi through your legs and do a circle. Then bring the poi back in front and continue with the Waist Wrap.

You'll need: **Waist Wrap**, **Through Your Legs**.

Crouch and go slow here.

Give the poi a good flick to spin this circle.

Do a Waist Wrap. As your arms uncross in front of you, bring your hands lower so your left poi is ready to do...

...a circle through your legs, followed by...

...your right poi.

At its lowest point, bring your left poi back out from between your legs, followed by...

...your right poi. Then just continue with the Waist Wrap.

ADVANCED MOVES

THE FIVE BEAT WEAVE

In the normal Weave, each hand does three circles or beats. In the Five Beat Weave each hand does *five* beats. Your right hand does an extra circle by staying on your right for a beat longer than usual, and another extra circle as your hands uncross on your left. Then your left hand mirrors this. The extra circles done by your right hand are shown below.

You'll need: **Weave**, and extra elbows.

> Next, as your left hand is about to come over the top of your right hand to your right side, let it do the extra circle on your left that you've just done on your right with your right hand. Then uncross on your right, which adds the fifth extra circle of your left hand.

Do a Weave. As your right hand is about to pass over your left hand to the left side of your body...

...instead let it point *under* your left hand to do yet *another* circle on your right, under your left arm. As your left poi comes down...

...start to take it to the left side of your body while the right hand is still bent around your left hand finishing the extra circle on your right.

As your right poi comes down, it follows your left poi to your left side. Let your hands...

...uncross, which adds a circle to the Weave (the fifth circle of your right hand). You're now back in the Weave, ready to do the extra circles with your left hand.

Again, each hand does five beats instead of the usual three. Your right hand bends back over your left hand to do an extra circle on your right. Then your hands uncross on your left, which adds another extra circle because your hands get to your left side more crossed than usual. Then it's all mirrored, this time with your left hand doing the extra circles. It can be a bit tangleful at first!

You'll need: **Backwards Weave**.

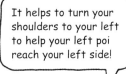

It helps to turn your shoulders to your left to help your left poi reach your left side!

Do a Backwards Weave. As your right hand is about to pass to your left...

...instead bend it back *over* your left hand to do another circle on your right...

...over your left hand. As the left poi comes up, start to take it to your left side...

...followed by your right poi as it comes up. Let your hands...

...uncross (which adds a 5th circle to the Weave). You're now back in the Backwards Weave, ready to do the same extra circles with your left hand.

Only half the move is shown here - the other half is a mirror of this half, with your left hand doing one extra circle on your left, over your right hand, and one as your hands uncross on your right.

SMALL CIRCLES

The poi spin Small Circles, one on each side of you, in opposite directions. The poi spin in split time, so that one poi reaches the bottom of its circle half a beat after the other poi.

You'll need: **Small Circles** (opposite directions), **Small Circles** (split time).

The poi spin in opposite directions, but they spin in split time, so one poi reaches the bottom of its circle half a beat after the other poi. The rhythm is the same as it is in split time when the poi are spinning in the same direction (page 28). Spinning in split time in opposite directions is easier to *do* than to imagine!

To get into split time from parallel time for any move, speed up one poi so it reaches the bottom of its circle half a beat before the other poi.

In parallel time in opposite directions, (like in the Butterfly, or the Small Circles on page 50), the poi pass each other at the top and bottom of their circles. But...

...in split time in opposite directions (as shown here) the poi pass each other at the *sides* of their circles. This makes the pattern look very unusual.

Spin a Small Circle in opposite directions. Then speed up one poi by half a circle so that it reaches the bottom of its path half a beat after the other poi. The rhythm feels exactly like spinning poi in split time in the same direction (page 28). The only difference is that the poi are now spinning in opposite directions.

GETTING INTO IT

The poi spin a Butterfly, but the poi reach the bottom of their circles half a beat apart, instead of at the same time. Here an inwards Split Butterfly is shown. Instead of one hand staying on top, the top hand constantly changes. You'll need: **Butterfly**, **Small Circles** (split time).

THE TRICK

Start with forwards circles in split time. Keeping the timing, gradually bend the planes until you are doing an inwards Butterfly in split time (in the wall plane).

Your left hand is on top, and passes...

...in front of your right hand as the left poi goes down. Your right hand comes up...

...on top of your left, and passes...

...in front of your left hand as your right poi goes down. Now back to picture 1.

Your hands bounce to the left and then to the right, instead of up and down. When they bounce to the right, your left hand is on top. As they bounce to the left, your right hand comes on top.

To do an outwards split Butterfly, start from *backwards* split time circles. This time your hands take turns to go *under* each other. Soon you'll be able to skip the 'getting into it' bit.

THE SPLIT BUTTERFLY TURN

From an inwards Split Butterfly you turn 180° into an outwards Split Butterfly, and then turn 180° back into an inwards Split Butterfly again. It's shown here as a Non-Turning Turn so that you can see the poi all the time.
You'll need: **Split Butterfly** (inwards and outwards).

Your poi move behind you as your right poi goes down and your left poi comes up. Weird!

Here your right poi is about to pass *outside* your left poi, so your right hand reaches around your left.

Start from an inwards Split Butterfly.

As the poi move to your left, start to turn your body to your left, and as your right poi comes down...

...take both poi behind you...

...so you're now doing an outwards Split Butterfly.

Your right poi touches down in front of you first - then your left.

Start from an outwards Split Butterfly.

As the poi go to the right, start to turn your body to the right, and...

...as your right poi comes down bring both poi back in front of you...

...into an inwards Split Butterfly.

Try this turning to the right as well. A nice effect is to turn to your left and back again (as shown here) followed immediately by turning to your right and back again.

You can also try this as a proper turn, instead of as a Non-Turning Turn as shown here.

THE YIN YANG

From split time Small Circles in opposite directions you turn 180° whilst doing a carry in split time. You finish with Small Circles. It's shown here as a Non-Turning Turn.
You'll need: **Carry Turn** (from forwards and backwards), **Small Circles** (opposite directions, split time).

Start with some split time Small Circles in opposite directions. Your left poi is spinning backwards. As your left poi comes up...

As you do the carry, it helps to think of the poi as tracing the shape of an eye, starting from one corner.

...turn 90° bringing your left poi up in a big carry and your right poi down in a carry in front of your legs.

As your left poi comes down, finish turning the last 90°, and as the poi pass each other...

...scoop them into small circles in split time. The hand that was spinning forwards in picture 1 is now spinning backwards.

The Yin Yang is actually the Carry Turns done in split time and in opposite directions! For more on changing the timing and direction of a trick, see pages 115-117.

Every trick you learn can be done in the four ways shown here with the Reel. The next few pages use examples to show you how to change the timing or direction of a trick, so you can work out these four variations of every move, from easier moves (like doing the Waist Wrap in same direction, *parallel time*) to more complicated ones (like doing the Weave in *opposite directions*, split time!). Working out these variations can be tricky, and can take a lot of thought - but sometimes you do end up with a great new move.

SAME DIRECTION PARALLEL TIME

SAME DIRECTION SPLIT TIME

OPPOSITE DIRECTIONS PARALLEL TIME

OPPOSITE DIRECTIONS SPLIT TIME

Each of these variations can also be done in 'rewind' (pages 17, 39 & 70), so in fact you can do every trick in at least eight different ways!

SPLIT REEL TURN

To change a trick from parallel to split time, one poi has to reach the bottom of each circle half a beat before the other. The important question is which hand this is. The best way to find out is by trial and error. Other than this, each hand does exactly what it does in the parallel time version of the move - whether the move is in the same or opposite directions. Here the Reel Turn from forwards, which is in parallel time, has been changed to a split time trick using exactly this method.
You'll need: **Reel Turn**, **Split Reels**, **Small Circles** (split time).

Spin a forwards circle in split time. As your right poi comes down...

...start to turn 90° to your left. Your right hand leads (it's the first to do the circle behind you of the Reel Turn)...

...followed by...

...your left hand. As your right poi comes up in front of you...

...turn another 90° to your left, so you are now doing backwards circles in split time.

Try turning to your right as well (your left hand leads), and try it with the Reel Turn from backwards too.

This turn looks great done as a Continuous Turn (page 26) with a Split Reel Turn from backwards.

When you change a trick from same to opposite directions, one hand does exactly what it does when you do the trick in one direction (eg forwards), and the other hand does exactly what it does when you do the trick in the other direction (eg backwards). Here the Reel Turn is changed from a same direction trick to an opposite direction trick.
You'll need: **Reel Turn**, **Small Circles** (opposite directions).

> In this move, your right hand does what it usually does when you do a Reel Turn from *forwards* turning to your left.

> Yeah, and your left hand does what it usually does when you do a Reel Turn from *backwards* turning to your left.

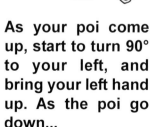

Start with Small Circles in opposite directions. Your left hand is spinning backwards circles.

You could also do this turn turning to your right, or with your right hand spinning backwards and your left hand spinning forwards.

As your poi come up, start to turn 90° to your left, and bring your left hand up. As the poi go down...

...let them spin a circle behind you.

As the poi go down, start to turn another 90°, so that...

...you end up doing Small Circles going in opposite directions by the time the poi reach the bottom.

To change a move in opposite directions to one in split time, just spin the poi in split time and choose a hand to lead.

PLACES TO SPIN A TRICK

It's useful to think of a trick as an object that you can move to different places around your body. Putting a trick behind your back is just one of the infinite number of places you can put a move. Here are a few ideas, using the humble Butterfly and the more complex Waist Wrap as examples.

MOVING THE BUTTERFLY

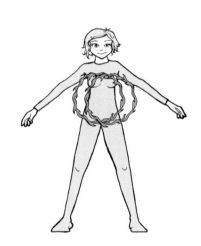

Here I've represented the Butterfly as two circles (one for each poi) with arrows to show the direction of spin. This is roughly the usual place where you spin the Butterfly.

You can move the Butterfly to anywhere around your body - imagine you'd drawn the circles on a bit of grease proof paper, so you can just move it around: up, down, diagonally, on its side, behind you...

...or into the side plane.

Most moves can be done in a few different ways in any one place. Here the Butterfly is in the same place as in picture 3, but the right hand is reaching across the back of the body, instead of across the front. When you move a trick to a new place, it's entirely up to you *how* your hands achieve this.

When you turn a Butterfly on its side the poi cross at the sides of their circles, so you end up spinning in split time.

MOVING THE WAIST WRAP

When you move a trick, you want the *shape* of the trace to stay the same. You also want the *direction* and *timing* to stay the same - so if a trick is in follow time with the poi spinning in the same direction, the trick will still be in follow time with the poi spinning in the same direction once you've moved it. Choose some tricks you like, and see if you can move them to a new place. The tricky part is working out how to move your hands so that you can spin the trick in the new place! This can take a lot of thought and trial and error - and bear in mind that not every move can be done in every place: for example a Big Circle can't be spun behind your back in the wall plane, because your arms just won't bend that way! Moving a trick to behind your back is dealt with in more detail on the next few pages.

The Waist Wrap: A circle behind your left hip, one in front of your belly button, a circle behind your right hip, and a carry in front. The poi spin these circles in follow time (page 96). Here I've shown the trace smaller than it would actually be.

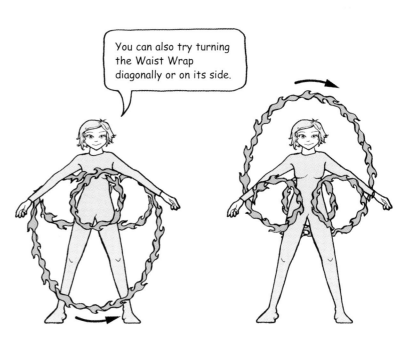

You can also try turning the Waist Wrap diagonally or on its side.

If you turn a trick *upside down*, it will seem like the direction has changed, so you start by your left hip with your left hand (which still leads) spinning *inwards* instead of outwards. An inwards Butterfly would become an outwards Butterfly.

When you put a move that is in the wall plane *behind* your body, the circles that were behind are now in front, and the ones that were in front are now behind (page 124).

119

BEHIND THE BACK (BTB)

BEHIND THE BACK BACKWARDS WEAVE: ONE HAND

When you move a trick from in front of your body to behind your body, the poi stay in the same planes. If the trick is in the side planes, your hands move to behind your body. If the trick is in the wall planes, circles that were in front of your body are now behind your body, and circles that were behind are now in front. Not all tricks can be done behind your body, because your arms often just won't bend that way. For example a Big Circle in the wall plane can't be done behind your back.

This is an example of a trick in the side plane moved to behind your back. Most people find the Backwards Weave easier to do behind the back than the Weave. Start by learning each hand on its own first: the poi spin backwards, and each hand spins one beat on its own side and two on the far side - three circles in total, just like with the normal Backwards Weave - but your hands cross from side to side *behind* your body, instead of in front.
You'll need: **Backwards Weave**.

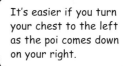

It's easier if you turn your chest to the left as the poi comes down on your right.

Start with your right hand empty and behind your back. Spin a backwards circle with your left hand, and...

...as the poi goes down, start to bring it over your right arm to your right side...

...to spin a backwards circle on your right. As the poi comes down...

If you find this tricky, practice the circles on your right side on their own. Careful not to point the poi too far away from or too close to your body.

You need to turn your right shoulder away from the incoming poi as the poi comes up, so the poi doesn't hit your right shoulder in the next picture.

Aim to keep the circles neatly in the side planes, not slanting away from your body too much.

The next step is to turn the page and try the full move with a stick instead of with poi. Put a ribbon on one end of your stick: this end represents the white poi. To start, hold the stick as shown here: palms facing each other, thumbs up, and fingers pointing away from you.

...uncross and recross your arms so your right hand is *underneath* your left hand as the poi comes up to start its third circle.

Now try these three circles with your right hand, so it spins one circle on your right, one on your left *over* your left hand, and one on your left *under* your left hand.

As the poi goes down, take it back to your left side, and start to uncross your arms on your left side...

...taking your left arm out from under your right, so you are back at picture 1.

Turn over and follow the pictures. The picture above is just after picture 6 overleaf. Do the motions without letting go of the stick or re-arranging your grip. The BTB Weave is much easier after this exercise, which gets your body to make the right movements.

BEHIND THE BACK BACKWARDS WEAVE

This is just like the Backwards Weave, but your hands cross from side to side *behind* your back. It's a tricky move, and may take time for your arms to get flexible enough to reach, and for you to get a good idea of what's going on behind you! It might also make your arms a little sore to begin with. Give it a bit of time, and when you need to, put the poi down and try again the next day.

You'll need: **BTB Backwards Weave: one hand**, lots of patience.

You need to turn your shoulders to the left as you do this, so the poi doesn't hit your shoulder.

Start with your right hand behind your back, and spin a backwards circle with your left hand. As the poi comes down...

...start your right poi spinning a backwards circle on your left side (chasing your left poi)...

...and bring your left poi down *over* your right hand to spin a backwards circle on your right side, followed by...

...your right poi. Then uncross your arms...

...taking your right hand out from under your left...

If you're hitting yourself, try turning a bit more. It can also help to keep your hands a little distance from your back, rather than touching your back - and turn to page 27 for even more help.

Your left hand stays on your right side, spinning its third circle.

You need to turn your shoulders to the right as you do this, so the poi doesn't hit your shoulder.

..and recross with your right arm coming over your left arm as the right poi goes down...

It helps to keep your fingers curled so the poi strings don't snag on your fingers.

...to spin a circle on your left, followed by...

...your left poi as it goes down.

Uncross your arms on your left, so that your left hand comes out from under your right hand...

...to go down over your right hand to the right side of your body again - just as in picture 2.

Eventually you won't need to turn your body as much as shown here.

BEHIND THE BACK WAIST WRAP

Like the Waist Wrap, your poi spin in split time in the same direction, spinning three circles at waist height (starting by your left hip) and then carrying back to the start. Your left hand still leads - but the circles that were behind you are now in front, and the ones that were in front are now behind! This means that the carry is quite small, because your arms can't spin very big circles behind your back. You'll need: **Waist Wrap**, body armour.

> At this point it helps to bend your torso away from your poi, and stick out your left hip.

Start with both hands by your left hip, your right hand reaching across behind your body. Spin a circle in front of your left hip with your left hand...

...followed by your right hand, which is *under* your left. As your left poi comes down...

...take it *over* your right hand to spin a circle behind you, followed by...

...your right poi. Your hands uncross...

It helps to keep your fingers curled so the poi strings don't snag on your fingers.

At this point it helps to bend your torso away from your poi, and stick out your right hip.

...and recross behind your back, with your right hand now on top. As your left poi comes up, move it a bit more to your right, and...

It helps you reach if you turn your chest away from the poi as they spin in front of you.

...as it comes down let it spin a circle in front of your left hip, followed by...

...your right hand, which passes *over* your left. As your left poi comes up...

...carry it behind your back, followed by your right poi. Now back to picture 1.

The BTB Waist Wrap is like a Non-Turning BTB Weave Turn from backwards - just as the Waist Wrap is like a Non-Turning Weave Turn from forwards. If you've worked out the BTB Weave, you should be able to link it to the BTB Backwards Weave once you've learnt the BTB Waist Wrap.

THE FULL WAIST WRAP

In the Full Waist Wrap, you link the BTB Waist Wrap to the normal Waist Wrap in the middle of the third circle, so that you do (almost) six split time circles around your waist. The carry is not there any more in its full form. This is just one way you could link the two Waist Wraps.
You'll need: **Waist Wrap**, **BTB Waist Wrap**.

This is picture 2 of the BTB Waist Wrap.

Spin a Waist Wrap, (starting behind your left hip). When you get to the third circle, (shown above), your left hand does the third circle but your right hand, instead of doing the third circle...

...carries the poi behind you to your left, ready to do the first circle of the BTB Waist Wrap. As your left hand comes up, take it across the front of your body to your left side, and *over* your right hand...

...to begin the circle behind you of a BTB Waist Wrap (the second circle) whilst your right hand finishes the circle in front of your left hip (the first circle). Now continue with the BTB Waist Wrap.

Turn your torso away from the poi as it spins in front of your hip in picture 3. It might also help to push your left hip forwards a little.

This is picture 2 of the Waist Wrap.

When you get to the third circle of the BTB Waist Wrap, (the one in front of your right hip), your left hand does the third circle but your right hand, instead of doing the third circle...

...crosses in front of your body to your left hip to start the first circle of the Waist Wrap (the one behind your left hip). As your left hand comes up...

...take it behind your body to cross over your right hand and start the second circle of the Waist Wrap (the one in front of your belly button) whilst your right hand finishes the first circle behind you.

Try to link these two parts together continuously. If you find you are hitting yourself, look at page 27 for some tips.

THE DROUGHT

There comes a time when you run out of moves and ideas - the dreaded drought has set in! It always passes: sometimes it's just a case of putting your poi down for a few weeks. Or you can look for new inspiration...

You could explore the sections in this book that help you develop new ideas. Try developing a new style (pages 42 and 90) or developing new tricks (page 73) or work out new ways to do old tricks (pages 115 and 118). There are loads of tricks out there not covered in this book, and as you develop your poi spining, you'll notice that tricks are much more interrelated than they are shown to be in this book: you'll find many relationships I've not mentioned, and that tricks have similarities I've not covered. This will give you a whole new bunch of relationships to explore and invent with.

Or, grab some people to play with. You could set up a weekly workshop in your area if you have none. If you have been spinning with friends for a while, try meeting up with spinners from another part of the country: people in the same area tend to develop similar ideas because they feed off each other, but people in different areas and groups tend to develop different tricks, styles and ideas. Check the websites at the back of this book to find out when events are on and to make contact with people in your own or other areas.

You could also try a new discipline, like another circus skill or any other type of object manipulation, or some form of physical training (like dance or martial arts). Sometimes it helps to give you new ideas of things you can bring from one discipline to another - or it just gives you a break from poi for a bit!

If you've not done a show, do one, or develop one completely different from the one that you do (page 136). This will give you a new perspective on spinning.

Sometimes it's not just a new move you want - it's only a whole new way of spinning that will satisfy you. There are a whole set of concepts not mentioned in this book. Mostly they involve breaking the rules you've mastered. So, think of the rules of poi and try breaking them - Must the poi spin round your hand or shoulder? Must they never wrap round each other? Must you never touch the string? You never know - you might come up with something special. (If you do, be sure to tell me about it so I can put it in the next book!)

Have fun!

FIRE SPINNING

Ah, the beautiful traces of whirling flames against the darkness!

Twirling fire holds a great thrill, and fortunately is not much more difficult than spinning ordinary poi. You don't have to be a pro to spin fire - but you do need to be very comfortable linking a number of tricks together, and *very* respectful of the dangers of fire spinning. Yes, I don't mean to alarm you, but fire spinning is **dangerous!** Obviously, this is part of its attraction, but you don't want to actually burn yourself or anyone else: it's more than a bit painful! The risk is not only setting things on fire, but also getting tangled in the chains which will give you some nasty burns.

If this is your first time spinning fire..
At least near the start of your fire career you don't want to be inventing, learning new things or just losing yourself in the flow when you're spinning fire, or you risk getting yourself into some nasty tangles. So before you light up for the first time, read the next few sections on fire safety, and then run through your repertoire to remind yourself of what moves you are going to do and to be sure you can link them smoothly.

Next, practice with your unlit fire poi to get used to them. They'll feel a little different once lit because of the drag created by the flames, but this warm up is still calming! Make sure you are spinning your unlit poi somewhere that is brightly lit: they are very hard to see in the dark, and it is likely that someone will walk into them. (Ouch!)

When you first light up it's a good idea to start in daylight (when the flames are not so bright and worrying!) - perhaps near dusk, and keep spinning as night falls so that almost without noticing you are spinning fire in the pitch black. This also gets you used to the noise of the flames, before you get to the point where you can't see much!

The next few pages discuss all the bits and bobs you'll need to know to spin fire as safely as possible. Don't take it lightly (ho ho!) - be as safe as you possibly can.

Fire poi are made of a kevlar wick, a metal chain, and a good strong handle.

The **wick** soaks up the fuel like a sponge. The more kevlar, the bigger and longer lasting the flame will be - but also the heavier your poi will be. When you light up, it's the fuel that burns (rather than the wick), but the wick blackens a bit, and will eventually fray and get a bit loose, at which point it needs replacing. There are three main designs for the wick, and they each give the poi a different 'feel' when you spin, so which one you use is down to personal preference. The monkey fist and cathedral stacked wick also hold more fuel for less weight than the wrapped wick.

There are three popular types of **chain**, and different people prefer different ones. Cable is lighter than the others, and some people find that ball chain is the best for wraps. The best metal for the chain and the other metal parts of your poi is aluminium, which is a poor conductor of heat so it won't burn you as quickly as say steel or brass.

The **handle** should be made of something strong that doesn't soak up fuel: Leather or imitation leather are both good options.

You should always attach a **safety loop** to your fire poi. You wear the safety loop around your wrist, so if you lose your grip on the poi they don't fly off and knock someone out! The loop should be a little loose on your wrist (you don't want to cut off your blood supply) and should be made of something strong that doesn't soak up fuel easily.

Whether you buy or make your own poi, make sure the parts are all very strong and very securely attached, so that the poi doesn't break in mid spin.

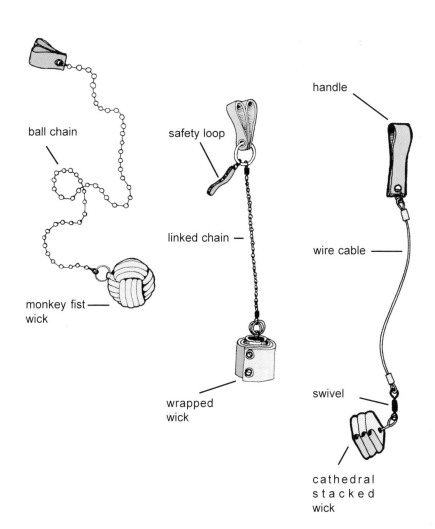

ball chain

monkey fist wick

safety loop

linked chain —

wrapped wick

handle

wire cable ——

swivel

cathedral stacked wick

BEFORE YOU START SPINNING FIRE...

FUEL

The best fuel to use is **paraffin** (**kerosene** in the US). It doesn't ignite too easily so it's not going to accidentally explode. It is quite smoky but burns with a cool flame, so the wicks can make brief contact with you without burning you badly. **Lamp oil** is the same as paraffin except it is highly toxic so don't let anyone fire-eat with it.

Lighter Fuel and **Coleman's Camping Fuel** (available in the US) are less smoky and have very bright flames - but are a little too volatile to be safe to use on their own, and have hotter flames. Because they ignite very quickly it's nice to add a few drops to your wicks (after they've been dipped in parafin) so that they catch light instantly. Don't dip even *smouldering* wicks in a mixture containing lighter fuel or Coleman's Camping Fuel, as even this is enough to set it all on fire.

Don't ever use petrol! Petrol (Gasoline in the US) is highly explosive and difficult to put out. It really is too dangerous to even think about. If you are considering any other fuels, check them out thoroughly on the websites on page 141 before you buy them.

FUEL CONTAINER

This should be a manufactured metal or plastic fuel container, clearly marked (so that no one mistakes it for water!) with a well fitting lid, and a neck wide enough to dip your wicks into.

CLOTHES

Leather, untreated cotton and your own skin are the best things to wear. Keep away from fleece, wool, plastics, artificial fibres and anything textured as these will catch fire easily and may melt onto you. (Ouch!) Your clothes should be close fitting with no tassles or loose threads. Also, make sure your hair is tied back and covered: hair will catch fire at the slightest contact with your fire poi.

ASSISTANT

Arrange for someone to watch nearby with a wet towel, fire blanket or dry chemical fire extinguisher who knows how and when to use them, in case you do get tangled or set fire to anything. They can also tell you if you've set yourself on fire - when you are spinning there is so much fire around you that it can be hard to tell for youself!

VENUE

Out doors, spin somewhere that has lots of open space and an even floor so you don't trip or fall over. Bring a fire blanket, and obey restrictions that prevent you starting forest fires. If you're going to swing indoors, check that the venue has a fire licence and that you won't be spinning on carpet. Cover the floor in sand so it doesn't get slippery with parafin, and have sand buckets, fire extinguishers or fire blankets to hand. The ceiling should be high and the place well ventilated, and check there are no drapes or hangings near you.

AUDIENCE

Make sure people nearby are aware of the space you'll be using and aren't going to walk into you! Before you start, check where your audience is and move them if you have to. In busy places and indoors you'll need to cordon off an area to spin in, and you may even need security people to keep the audience out of your way.

INSURANCE

You need at least third party public liability insurance to spin fire - you don't want to end up with a bill of millions should an accident occur with someone else or someone else's property!

1. Check your poi are in a good state of repair, especially that screws or links (and the safety loops) aren't loose. You don't want your poi flying off in mid spin. Then put the safety loops around your wrists.
2. Check your assistant has a wet towel, and knows you are ready to spin. You can agree a code word between you that they will shout if you cach fire - the word 'fire' is said a lot in places where people spin fire, and you don't want too many false alarms!
3. Dip your wick into the fuel until it stops bubbling. Hold the wick over the fuel container until it stops dripping, and then close your fuel container properly, even if you're going to use it again.
4. Find a spot where no one will be spinning and shake your poi to get rid of excess fuel, so it doesn't fly off your poi once the fuel is lit.
5. Check you have no fuel on you - you may need to wipe your hands and the poi handles.
6. Move to a new place to spin that's at least a few meters from your fuel container and the place where you shook off the excess fuel.
7. Hold one poi up by the handle and light it by holding a flame under it. You can light the second poi off the first one, holding both poi by the handles. If you're using a lighter, don't put the lighter in your pocket as it might explode if you hit it with your poi. (Erk!)
8. *Spin!*
9. When the flames get very low, spin them fast to put them out. It's best not to wait for them to go out on their own as this damages the wicks when they start to smoulder. It's also not a good idea to blow them out as they do sometimes backfire. Value those eyebrows!
10. As soon as the poi are out, re-dip them in the fuel even if you are not going to use them again. This stops the wick smouldering, which damages the wick. (If you're using lighter fluid, crush the wicks with a cloth. Use your feet to crush so that you don't burn your hands.)
11. If you're going to light up again, let your poi cool for a few minutes first. If not, let your wicks cool all the way down and then put them away in a bag that isn't going to let fuel leak everywhere.

...you splash fuel on yourself: If you splashed on your clothes, change your clothes before you light up, as only a machine wash will get enough fuel out of your clothes to prevent them catching fire. If you splashed fuel on your skin, just wipe yourself off. If you splashed fuel in your eyes, hold your eyes open and splash cold running water in your eyes for fifteen minutes. Then get medical attention immediately. You'll probably be fine, but some fuels can damage your eyes so it's best to see a doctor just in case.

...You swallow some fuel: (Now why would you want to do that?) Don't induce vomiting but seek medical attention immediately.

...Your poi get tangled around your arms: Get your assistant to smother the flames, then untangle the poi by gingerly holding the wicks (which won't be too hot) taking care not to touch any metal.

...Your poi tangle round each other: Put them on the floor, handles as one end and wicks at the other, and untangle from the handles.

... You get burned: Slight burns put under cold running water for fifteen minutes. Worse burns put under cold running water for fifteen minutes and seek medical attention immediately. Burns get infected very easily so keep the area very clean until you get medical help.

COLOURED FLAME

Different chemicals can be used to colour flame - but very few are safe, affordable and readily available. One chemical that is is **Boric acid**. This is available from chemists and gives a green flame. It won't dissolve in paraffin, but you can use **100% ethanol**. Add a couple of teaspoons of the Boric acid to the fuel, mix, dip and glow!

Don't use Methylated spirits as a solvent, (even though it is mostly ethanol) because it releases toxic vapours and is damaging to your eyes and other parts of you. It also deteriorates your wicks.

And of course, don't experiment with other chemicals unless you know they're safe.

SPARKLE

Now this is a real treat, though it never seems to last more than about a minute:

You can attach a bunch of **sparklers** to the heads of your fire poi with some tightly wound wire (so they don't come off) and light them. Be very careful of the tips - they're super hot. You can also use **Wire wool**, like you use for scrubbing dishes. This sparkles once you get it swinging. Bind it well to your wicks with lots of wire, dip your wicks as usual and light up. Tada! The human catherine wheel! Be very wary of the bits of glowing wool that fly off your poi - they are hot and could set fire to things, so be far from your audience, extra careful of your surroundings, and wear eye protection if you can.

Don't ever use fireworks or other pyrotechnics, which are extremely dangerous. You've heard the horror stories - stay away from them or do a pyrotechnics course so you know how to use them safely.

GLO-POI

You can attach glow sticks to your poi for a colourful light show. Many poi manufacturers also make glo-poi that are battery powered or re-chargeable: check out the websites at the back of this book.

nunchuks (martial arts)
You hold one end and spin them, and do damage.

kusari kama (martial arts)
Spun exactly like poi - but the blade at the end hurts more when you hit yourself.

There are hundreds of objects similar to poi used around the world - Poisters aren't the only ones to spend time spinning things! Here are a few examples from juggling, martial arts, and other performance arts.

clubs (juggling)
See page 89 for more on this. You'll be pleased to know you can get fire clubs too.

gymnastic ribbons (rhythmic gymnastics)
These are on a rigid stick, but the ribbons make traces much like poi. You need to be able to put both feet behind your head whilst somersaulting in the air to use these properly.

meteor
An old Chinese weapon, now a performance art. You use these as if they were a cross between staff and poi.

batton (US performance art)
A small weighted stick for spinning between your fingers and hands, throwing and rolling along your body whilst wearing a spangly outfit.

flags
Big rectangles of light fabric, weighted at one corner. You hold them at one corner and then treat them like poi - but they're more difficult because they fold themselves up if you're not careful.

staff (juggling)
A big stick (or two) up to 5 feet long, often with fire wicks at either end, for spinning, throwing and rolling along your body by some bonfire in the countryside.

135

CHOREOGRAPHY

Choreographing a show is very different to just letting yourself spin spontaneously. It can feel a bit limiting at first to tie yourself to a choreographed piece, but it lets you add energy, climaxes, comedy and atmosphere that you can't achieve without careful planning.

Any poister of any level can choreograph a brilliant piece, because putting on a good show is more about how you *present* what you can do than how many difficult, technical moves you can pull off.

There's a million ways to put together a show, so I've chosen one of my favourite ways to do it, and split it into two parts: the first part explains how to get the outline of your show, and you can stop at that if you want to. The second part explains the secrets of a good performance. Finally there are some extra pointers for putting together a group performance.

How long it takes to put together a show depends entirely on what you want to achieve. At least two weeks is a good idea, but the most impressive shows have usually been perfected over months of performing and tweaking the piece. There's no better way to learn than to perform it.

1. IMAGINE...
First, sit down and imagine your act. Think of how you would want it to be if it was at its most perfect, and then sit back and watch yourself perform. What are you wearing? What colours is the show? How do you move? What's the music like? What's the atmosphere like? Getting a clear picture of what you want from your show is a great way to start - and very inspiring too!

2. GET YOUR TUNE (if you're using one!)
Now get some music that suits your show, and is between 1 to 6 minutes long (so your show doesn't go on too long for your audience!). It's useful to have a piece that has a lot of variety in it - for example different noises, or fast and slow bits. Stay away from songs with lots of lyrics - it tends to detract attention from your skill. Also, a dramatic end to the music is usually more effective than a fade out. Most importantly, it should be a piece you enjoy - after all, you're going to spend a lot of time listening to it!

3. CHOOSE YOUR MOVES
Next, write a list of the tricks you can do. Leave out anything that you can't do at least fifteen times in a row, to be sure you're only using tricks you're confident with. Then, put a star by the tricks that you particularly enjoy, or that you think look particularly pretty, dramatic, expressive or funny - depending on the type of piece you're doing. You can always use a mirror (a big one!) to help you decide which moves look good.

Think of the audience you will be performing to to help you choose your moves. For example, if you're performing to other poisters, technical moves will be appreciated, but if you're performing to people who don't spin poi some technical moves will be lost on them: the Five Beat Weave, for example, looks just like the Three Beat Weave if you're not a poister. This doesn't mean you shouldn't use it, but it's not going to be the move that gets the cheers! Other technical moves they will love: behind the back stuff for example, if you build it up enough! If you don't feel you know much technical stuff yet, don't let that stop you! It's how you present your moves that counts - and simple moves can be the most effective.

4. WRITE OUT YOUR MUSIC

It's useful to write your music out using your own made up symbols, especially if you are doing a group performance. This means you don't have to rewind your music all the time, and you get a much clearer picture of how to fit things in, or why something isn't working. This is just an outline of the main cues and changes in the music - you don't want to write out every note! Using a cross to represent each beat is useful, and next to the crosses draw your symbols. As you choreograph your piece, you can write down which moves you are going to do next to the place you are going to do them. Two bars from a piece are shown below.

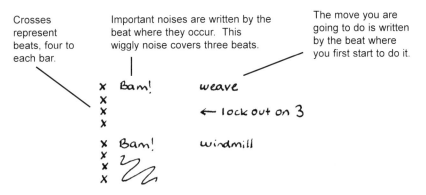

Crosses represent beats, four to each bar.

Important noises are written by the beat where they occur. This wiggly noise covers three beats.

The move you are going to do is written by the beat where you first start to do it.

Once you've written in your moves, feel free to move bits around if you think they'd fit the music better in another place - nothing's ever written in stone!

5. PUT YOUR MOVES TO THE MUSIC

Next you've got to put some moves together, and match them to the music. Get the outline first - you can perfect it over time. Of course you can have a bit that is non-scripted, and come back to your script after a bit of spontaneous spinning.

Start at a point in the music (it doesn't have to be the beginning - you can add that on later), choose a move you like and do it for four beats (assuming your music is in 4/4 time). Then choose another move and do it for four, and so on until you have the whole piece. You don't need to hold every move for four, but it's a good way to start if this is your first time choreographing. Then you can add some variation to your four beats - for example, if you are spinning the Weave for four beats, you could do a Lock Out on the third beat.

Match your moves to the music as much as possible, so that a stop in the music is matched with a Stop, or a wiggly sound is matched with a wiggly pattern or body movement. Also, keep the plane of the poi facing audience most of the time, so they can see the full trace.

For your starting trick, it's often worth using a very high impact body movement - something huge and very visually effective. When you finish, again use the most exciting trick you can, and then stop your poi (page 83) so you end up in a dramatic pose, and bow to end.

Next, play with the moves you have chosen to get a better effect with each one. A particular stance might enhance a move, or speeding it up. Have a look at the suggestions on page 42 for some more ideas.

6. PRACTICE AND TWEAK!

Practice your piece to the music, making sure your transitions between moves are very smooth, and that you have the time you need to make these transitions. Make any changes you feel your piece needs in order to fit the music well. Then you're ready!

Here are some ideas to help you to make your show even more effective!

VARIETY

To keep the audience gripped, you'll need lots of variety in every aspect of your show, from the speed you spin at to whether you are staying in the same place or running around. Here's a few ideas:

Use the space: move all around the stage, using the back, the front and the sides (or front corners) - although you probably want to use the front/middle as your main focus. Using big open body movements and pointing your toes (!) also makes you take up the space.

Use big as well as small patterns: you can even change the length of your poi in mid-spin to enhance this. Long poi work well after small poi because they're more dramatic. You can also use space by playing with the height of your tricks, using high as well as low tricks, or stretching up as well as kneeling down.

Vary the timing, including at least parallel and split time. Breaking into follow time works well after spinning in parallel time for a bit because it looks more hectic.

Use very different patterns: for example, the Weave makes a very different pattern to, say, a Split Pirouette or the Sweep.

Vary the speed you spin at: starting a trick slow and getting very fast is a good one - so is spinning slow and then double time for a couple of beats before going back to spinning slow. Slowing down (or stopping) also gives you quieter moments so you can build up again and again.

Stopping completely for a couple of beats is also great, contrasting with your spinning, especially if you have an effective stance and your stop ties in with a pause in the music.

Use different stances for different tricks, and exaggerate them as much as possible, making each stance as interesting as possible. The stance should include your whole body, especially your feet and legs. Use a mirror to help you decide what works.

INTERACTING WITH THE AUDIENCE

Look *at* the audience (even if you can't see them), not over their heads or at the floor. If you look at the audience, you are letting them into your private world, not pretending that they aren't there, and this makes them involved in your piece, so they can't look away!

Looking at the audience takes courage and practice. It's easiest to choose particular moments in your piece when you will make eye contact with the audience, whether to smile at them, nod at them, frown at them or to look at them sadly - depending on the nature of your piece. Then practice these moments as part of your piece every time you rehearse.

ASKING FOR APPLAUSE

Usually, you want the audience to applaud as often as possible during your piece - and massively at the end. You should aim to start with a bang, have lots of bangs in the middle, and end with the biggest bang! If you make them applaud (or laugh) near the start of your piece, you'll have warmed them up and they'll be feeling positive about your show.

One way to get a clap is to build anticipation and then do something fabulous. For example, if you do a move slowly, then faster and faster and finally super fast, you'll probably get a big clap. Or, if a move looks like it's difficult, build up to it: almost do it, almost do it again, (letting the audience know you're trying to do something hard) and then finally...do it! Wow! What an achievement! You can also *surprise* the audience: do something quieter and then burst into something massive and impressive.

Use your face and body to ask for applause at the climax moments. Nodding or grinning at the audience just at the moment when you perform the great feat lets the audience know that something amazing is happening. Also, when you do a move or pose that you want the audience to applaud, hold it for at least four beats to give the audience time to respond - with wild applause! You could also do something fantastic and then stop spinning, and give a big grin. They'll love it.

KNOW YOUR PIECE INSIDE OUT
Have your piece very well practiced so you can cope with the extra pressure of being on stage. This means practicing it all - coming on stage, facial expressions, having lots of energy, bowing (hold your bow for between 5 - 10 secconds to give the audience time to clap), and leaving. Practice in your costume with the props you'll be using - and if you have a chance, practice in the space where you'll be doing the show, together with the people who'll be doing your lighting and music.

Have a plan of action for if you tangle. You'll probably know your piece well enough for this not to be a risk, but have a back-up plan just in case. You can make it a joke or pretend it is part of your piece. You can also have a spare set of poi incase of terrible tangles: if they're very different to the poi you've used so far in the show you can make it look like you meant to swap poi at this point.

DELIVER YOUR PIECE WITH LOADS OF ENERGY
Whatever type of show you do, you want to be literally bursting off the stage, so you need lots of energy! So, before you go on, warm up. Then, work yourself into the appropriate mindset: visualise your show as it would be in the ideal, to get your energy up, or give yourself a little pep-talk. And, if you enjoy your piece, it will come across with even more energy. Your props and costume should also aim for the highest visibility, to help give you lots of impact.

IF YOU WANT TO TAKE CHOREOGRAPHY VERY SERIOUSLY
To produce a great piece takes time and experience: first you make a piece, then you try it out on audiences and refine it. You can also video yourself so you can watch your performance, and get the opinion of friends. If a part of the show fell flat, think how to replace it with a moment of drama. There are ways to make an audience applaud any trick - it's all about how you present it! You'll learn more and more what works: doing it is the best way to learn - second only to watching other people do it! You can also get the help of a professional choreographer or do a choreography course.

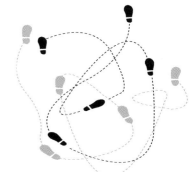

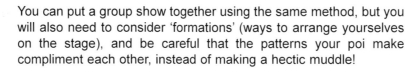

You can put a group show together using the same method, but you will also need to consider 'formations' (ways to arrange yourselves on the stage), and be careful that the patterns your poi make compliment each other, instead of making a hectic muddle!

It's usually most interesting if you use a variety of formations. Some formations for a group of four performers are shown on this page. You can move about the stage whilst holding a formation, or move to get from one formation to another. Come up with a variety of ways to move between formations, and make sure you allow for the time it will take to get from one formation to another.

Most formations are symmetrical in some way. The patterns your poi make are less confusing if they are also symmetrical in some way - for example if the two people outside spin one trick whilst the two people in the middle spin another trick. If people in the group are doing different tricks from each other at one time, it helps if the difference is very clear - for example very high vs very low tricks, very big vs very small tricks, or tricks with very different patterns.

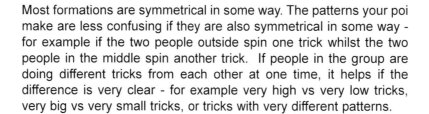

In some formations some people are obscured, because they are behind other people. This is fine so long as the patterns your poi make are clear and complement each other - for example if you all do exactly the same move, or if you do the same move at different heights, with people at the back spinning higher than people at the front. It can be quite effective to experiment with obscuring and revealing people as you move between different formations.

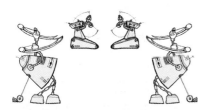

If you need one or all of the performers to change direction, for example from same direction to opposite directions, you'll need time to change directions (in this case to stop a poi). This change should also look good - let it be a part of the show - don't hide it!

THE COMPLETE JUGGLER
Dave Finnigan
588 pages £10.00
ISBN 0 9513240 2 0

CHARLIE DANCEY'S ENCYCLOPAEDIA OF BALL JUGGLING
224 pages £14.95
ISBN 1 898591 13 X

CHARLIE DANCEY'S COMPENDIUM OF CLUB JUGGLING
248 pages £14.95
ISBN 1 898591 14 8

HOW TO RIDE YOUR UNICYCLE
Charlie Dancey
32 pages £4.95
ISBN 1 898591 18 0

CONTACT JUGGLING
James Ernest
100 pages £11.95
ISBN 1 898591 15 6

SPLITTING THE ATOM
and other Yo-Yo Stuff
Richie Windsor
48 pages £1.95
ISBN 1 898591 16 4

THE HYDROGEN BOMB
and even more Yo-Yo Stuff
Richie Windsor
40 pages £1.95
ISBN 1 898591 17 2

COURSES

Cosmos Jugglers:
Club Swinging and Pole Spinning Courses
Includes fire & UV swinging skills and choreographed performance, as well as workshops in other circus skills. Contact Anna Semlyen (nee Jillings) on: www.cosmosjugglers.co.uk

Apex Poi Spining Courses
Michal Kahn runs Beginners, Intermediate and 'Breaking the Rules' poi spinning courses in London, and a Choreography course for professional performers.
For further information, contact her on:
poicourses@juggler.net

BOOKS

The Rhythm and Life of Poi
Ngamoni Huata
Published by Harper Collins
ISBN 1 86950 273 6

Modern Club Swinging and Pole Spinning
Anna Jillings
ISBN 0 9513240 8 X
Order from Anna:
anna@semlyen.net

Club Swinging for Physical Exercise and Recreation
W.J. Schatz
Published by Brian Dube
ISBN 0 9176430 8 9

The Book of Club Swinging
Ben Richter
Published by Circustuff
ISBN 0 9520300 4 7

The Meteor Book
Rhys Thomas
Flaming Sparrow Press
ISBN 0 943292 26 3

WEBSITES

www.homeofpoi.com
A brilliant website visited by thousands of poi swingers worldwide. Includes poi lessons, diary of worldwide events, discussion pages, and a shop. It's also a great way to make contact with poisters and find workshops in your area.

www.firechains.com
Excellent sections on fire safety, constructing fire toys, photographing fire, non-fire ideas and a little teaching of moves.

www.spinage.org
Quality, stylish clothes with funky fire and poi characters printed on them. Also information on poi classes and events, as well as contemporary fire photographs and artworks.

www.globall.com
The website of Aerotech Projects, manufacturers of excellent quality rechargeable, programmable glow equipment, including glo-poi, glo-meteors, glo-clubs, glo-staff and glo-balls.

BRIEF INDEX OF TRICKS

Bold numbers refer to the most important entries.

INDEX OF TERMS AND CONCEPTS

You can use this to look up all you need to know about each concept!

ALL ABOUT MICHAL...

Michal Kahn started spinning poi sometime in the murky past, when a mere handful of poisters jostled for space in the English juggling workshops. Soon after, she began performing around England and is a performer in the London based troupe 'Apex'.

Secretly, however, she prefers teaching to performing - although she insists this has nothing to do with enjoying bossing people around. She has taught informal workshops for several years, and at present runs Beginners, Intermediate and 'Breaking the Rules' poi courses at various venues in London, as well as Choreography courses for professional performers.

One day, she decided it was high time there was a book on poi spinning and, after remarkably little deliberation, decided that she would like to spend a couple of months writing one. Although it took somewhat longer to complete than expected (about five times longer!) the result is now in your hands.

Michal is of the conviction that if she keeps her life as varied as possible, this will make her more interesting. Hence she has lived in various countries, and her hobbies include balloon modelling, list writing, juggling, organising stuff, doodling, biology, science fiction, books that come in at least seven volumes, and fluorescent plasticine. She also has a strange habit of photographing barbie dolls as if they were real people.

Like most sane people she hates washing the dishes and has discovered that, contrary to popular opinion, they do in fact wash themselves if you leave them for long enough - although her house-mates have tried to convince her that, strictly speaking, this is not how it happens at all.

You can contact Michal at poicourses@juggler.net if you're interested in courses, or if you know some particularly impressive balloon models.

poicourses@juggler.net   michal@juggler.net

ALL ABOUT LUCY...

hello

i think this might be the best recipe in the world

love from lucy x

p.s. if you've got a better one, please send it to me! x

Sophie's Chocolate Brownies

100g Butter
40g Cocoa powder
225g Caster sugar
1 tsp Vanilla Essence
50g Self-raising flour
50-100g Chopped walnuts or pecans

Heat your oven to 180 degrees c.
Grease a 20cm square cake tin and line the bottom with greaseproof paper.

In a saucepan, melt the butter over a low heat and add the cocoa powder.
In a separate bowl, beat the eggs and sugar together until they're thick and pale.
Add the chocolaty butter mixture and vanilla essence to the bowl and stir it together a little bit. Sift the flour in and add the nuts, mix it all together (now it looks how it should).
Pour it into the baking tin (and tap the tin on the surface a couple of times to spread it and get rid of trapped air).
Bake it for 30-35 minutes.
When you take it out of the oven, leave it in the tin for about 10 minutes, and then turn out onto a cooling rack.
It's easiest to cut into squares when it's cooled, but it's really hard to resist eating them while it's still hot 'cause it smells so irresistible.

My Grandma's Homemade Lemonade

(The measurements are imperial because it's very old.)
3 Lemons
1Lb Granulated Sugar
1.1/2 tsp Citric Acid
1 tsp Tartaric Acid
2 Pints of boiling water

Grate the zest from the lemons and juice them (if you put them in the microwave for about 20 seconds to warm, it gets a lot more juice) add the other ingredients and leave it to cool. Stir it every now and then to make sure the sugar dissolves.
Strain out the bits through a sieve and dilute it to drink.
It's really good chilled in the summer.

lucy.jane.b@virgin.net

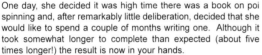